Yes, Francis!

Ways to Help the
Post-Pandemic World

PUBLISHED BY :

 Clear Faith Publishing
781 Caxambas Drive
Marco Island, FL 34145

ISBN: 978-1-940414-39-3

Cover & interior design by Doug Cordes
Cover art by Br. Mickey O'Neill McGrath, osfs

The mission of Clear Faith Publishing is to spread joy, peace and comfort through great writing about spirituality, religion and faith that touches the reader and serves those who live on the margins. Portions of the proceeds from this book are donated to organizations that feed, shelter, and provide counsel for those in need. For more information, please visit us at: www.clearfaithpublishing.com.

Yes, Francis!

WAYS TO HELP THE POST-PANDEMIC WORLD

Edited by Brennan Pursell

Foreword

BY FR. JIM GREENFIELD, OSFS

Avanti! This Italian word meaning "go forth" is a tagline of Pope Francis as he urges Christians to share their faith with enthusiasm and vitality, heaped with creativity and audacity. Cautioning us from the early days of his pontificate not to look like we just returned from a funeral as we go forth, he exhorts us to summon the courage to be truly happy. The essays in this book respond, "Yes, Francis!" as he challenges educational institutions to be places of encounter and dialogue within and beyond their walls—with people of other cultures and traditions and of different religions, so that a Christian humanism can consider the fuller reality of humanity today. "This sort of networking means making the school an educating community where teachers and students are brought together not only by the teaching curriculum, but also by a curriculum of life and experience that can educate the different generations to mutual sharing. This is so important so as not to lose our roots!" (*Veritatis Gaudium*, 4c).

The American scientist E. O. Wilson keenly observed: "We are drowning in information, while starving for wisdom. The world henceforth will be run by synthesizers, people able to put together the right information at the right time, think critically about it, and make important choices wisely."[1]

Now, more than ever, we need synthesizers—people who speak to us plainly and clearly—to help us not only begin, but also remain in conversations on topics that concern our common future. This is the networking that Pope Francis encourages, and, in that spirit, it is a pleasure to introduce the following essays, written by fourteen of my colleagues from the faculty at DeSales University in Center Valley, Pennsylvania, where I serve as president. DeSales is a Catholic, Salesian university dedicated to inspiring transformative learning through the liberal arts and professional studies by energizing our students to be who they are and be that well—as St. Francis de Sales said so pithily, yet powerfully.

The essays in this volume were written during the COVID-19 pandemic and flow from Pope Francis' book *Let Us Dream*. As a metaphor, dreaming helps us to look at what is all around us without letting familiarity breed contempt. These faculty dream about fresh possibilities for our national and world economy, the conduct of business both here and abroad, and the delivery of education in a world that has broken down the walls between online and in-classroom.

Embarking the universal church on a synodal path, Pope Francis has formally launched the two-year global consultation process leading to the 2023 Synod on Synodality with a call to look others in the eye and listen to what they have to say. In a homily, the pope said that Catholics taking part in the synodal path should strive to become experts in the art of encounter. Otherwise, as he said in *Fratelli Tutti*, "Life without fraternal gratuitousness becomes a form of frenetic commerce, in which we are constantly weighing up what we give and what we get back in return" (140). In the grace-filled moment prompted by this synodal experience, it is my hope that these essays can spark other Catholic university faculties to be a resource to parishes as they explore how local communities can advance the Gospel and live it with joy, which is another exhortation of Pope Francis.

As I write this Foreword, our world seems to be shifting from a global pandemic into the endemic stage of the COVID-19 virus—unless, God forbid, a new variant puts us back to square one. These nearly two years of sickness, death, economic constriction, and withdrawal have beckoned us toward a renewed solidarity. Pope Francis describes this in *Fratelli Tutti* as "a moral virtue and social attitude born of personal conversion [that] calls for commitment on the part of those responsible for education and formation" (114). I am grateful for my colleagues on the faculty at DeSales University, whose writings herein offer an unqualified, "Yes, Francis!" They highlight and synthesize the essential call of the Gospel for us to encounter the world with "the right information at the right time," as we make critically important choices for our shared future so that we can be who we are and be that well. *Avanti*!

Yes, Francis!

BY BRENNAN PURSELL

In 2020, the first full year of the COVID-19 pandemic, Pope Francis reminded all of us never to waste a crisis.

In *Let Us Dream: The Path to a Better Future*, Francis describes our current time as one of trial and reckoning. In such times, I think it is fair to say, people reveal their true colors through their thoughts, words, and actions. We see the whole spectrum of human behavior played out at large. Some build others up while others tear people down. Some work to better the lot of those less fortunate, and others focus solely on their own power and wealth, no matter the cost to others. The heroes in the COVID-19 crisis are those who have worked hard and given of themselves; the villains are the active dis-informers and the ruthless profiteers—and then there is that great lot in the middle who watch what is happening, dislike it, but keep on going as if nothing were any different than before, as long as they are OK.

Crises like the COVID-19 pandemic are a wake-up call, a grand occasion for us all to re-examine who we are and what we do, to diagnose societal and structural problems as well as disease, and to take steps now to make the future a bit better than the past. In the history of the globe, no country or collective was or is free of error. All self-declared utopias fail, usually in a rather short timeframe, and there are always areas for improvement wherever we look. Part of true patriotism is to be clear-eyed about our country's failings and actively work to remediate them. Strident claims of personal and collective superiority not only ring hollow but also reflect the presence of inner imbalance, defect, and distortion.

As the leader of the world's largest Christian church, Francis baldly states that Christianity is not about one's own faith and one's individual path to salvation, but about the teaching "that God loved me and gave himself up for me." We therefore need to see all other human beings as siblings in the one, great human family. "A Christian," Francis says, "will always defend individual rights and freedoms but can never be an individualist. A Christian will love and serve her country with patriotic feeling, but cannot be merely a nationalist."[1] He recommends that we reconcile solidarity in service with pursuit of profit, that we couple ethics with the economy, and that we strive for labor, healthcare, and education for all people.

This book is a response from faculty in business, healthcare, and education at DeSales University. Fourteen chapters look at systems and structures that COVID-19 has revealed to be in need of improvement—in some cases, dire. Against academic tradition, we authors have chosen to use our everyday names and dispense with middle initials, titles, and academic and professional degree acronyms. Our ideas stand for themselves. We identify problems, describe what they entail, and recommend solutions. Citations are relegated to endnotes, and we avoid jargon in order to make the conversation as broad and inclusive as possible. We speak from the heart as well as the mind.

In the section about Business and Economics, Sue McGorry encourages the marketing profession to treat the customer as a person in the fullest sense of the term. No human being can or should be reduced to a set of numbers. Chris Cocozza highlights provisions and loopholes in the US taxation system that allow the richest of the rich to avoid paying income tax and suggests ways to rectify that fundamental issue. Amy Scott describes the immensely jarring changes in the US labor market and predicts which will last and which will pass. Tahereh Hojjat calls out the grotesque inequities in US wealth distribution and suggests an approach to policy that looks at more than GDP per capita as a measure of success. Elisabeth Felten argues that the new reality of working from home is here to stay because of its extensive advantages for many individuals and families. My chapter is a plea that we adopt a data-based mindset when it comes to analyzing situations and making decisions, especially in our data-rich, digitized, and interconnected world.

In the Healthcare section, Stephen Carp shows how the COVID-19 crisis exposed the weak performance of the US healthcare system, the social and racial roots of its poor health outcomes, and the counter-productive politicization of basic scientific recommendations. Deborah Whittaker tells how DeSales nursing faculty and students adjusted instruction and work experience in the same spirit and footsteps of Florence Nightingale. Bobbie Morici highlights the fundamental importance of human interaction, connection, and touch in medicine, and how these need to be restored and strengthened in the pandemic's wake. Karen Peterson emphasizes joy in a nurse's work and several of the ways nurses taught, supported, and cared for others during the pandemic, not only in the fight against the virus itself, but also against depression and suicide. Jackie Ochsenreither's chapter highlights the soaring stress and immense mental and emotional burden among university students, both traditional and non-traditional: those with jobs and caregiver roles for children and other dependents, and those who suffered grief, loss, violence, and unemployment. Colleges and universities need to support their students in full awareness of their stations and situations in life.

In the Education section, Katrin Blamey details the turmoil that shuttered schools brought upon the country, the upheaval in the usual modalities for teaching young people, the fury hurled at school boards from parents with diametrically opposing views about how to proceed, and the precipitous fall in student learning in 2020–2021. Fortunately, she foresees a superbloom after the forest fire. The pandemic reveals the absolute, vital importance of the school as a societal institution, and the near universal need for a teacher to be at the center of each class. Human connection remains paramount in the teaching and learning process. Aidin Amirshokoohi and Mahsa Kazempour show how the pandemic caused an "infodemic," as mis- and dis-information distorted an already challenging flood of information about how best to avoid infecting oneself and others. They recommend that educators emphasize "scientific literacy" that includes scientific content and processes, their sociocultural context, and their application to global problems for informed decision-making. They also advocate that STEM instruction be as humanistic as it is scientific, for everyone's benefit, in accordance with the mission of DeSales University. Finally, Kevin Nadolski presents Pope Francis' vision of education, formulated for our times but also in full consistency with the teachings of his papal predecessors from the last century. For Francis, education should be centered on the human person, and, with the church, it should spread love, tenderness, and mercy to a world in desperate need.

COVID-19 will probably be with us for some time yet; this is not a repeat of the 1918 influenza, which more or less ran its course in fourteen months. COVID-19's Delta variant was demonstrably more contagious and damaging, rather than less so, and the world's roughly eight billion people offer ample opportunity for the virus to generate more variants, such as Omicron. The distribution of vaccines runs noticeably slower than the virus itself, which is no surprise, given its global reach. The hope is that the COVID-19 pandemic will subside and become an endemic disease, if we cannot manage to stamp it out completely, like we did with smallpox.

We hope you enjoy this shared work. If you find our ideas interesting, please engage us in dialogue. Let's widen the discussion. A closed conversation among professors really benefits no one but themselves—if that. Let's take on a project together. Bring us a challenge. The ivory tower model for universities only made sense as long as a tiny, exclusive elite attended them. These days, it's utterly irrelevant. We can make the world a better place to the extent that we work together.

CHAPTER 1

Market Reset: Respect the Customer as a Person

BY SUE MCGORRY

Emily Dickinson challenged us in her verse to see heaven on earth: to use the love God has shared with us to grow as human beings created in the image and likeness of God.

> Who has not found the heaven below
> Will fail of it above.
> God's residence is next to mine,
> His furniture is love.

In *Let Us Dream*, Pope Francis calls upon all of us to reexamine ourselves and our lives. Where is our path to the future post-pandemic? Can the chaos of upheaval reveal a richer, more robust society embracing humanity in its full beauty as bestowed upon us by God?

In March of 2020, the economy and world as we knew it came to a standstill. Fear gripped every household, school, and organization like a vise. Hospitals and medical facilities scrambled to serve: to serve as best as they possibly could with limited resources, faulty equipment, and limited medication and protection. While we began to don masks, we might not have realized that this horrific pandemic, which stole the lives of so many and crushed souls and spirits, could also enable us to unmask many of the inequities and injustices in society today.

Pope Francis said in a recent homily, "The meaning of life is found in our response to God's offer of love. And that response is made up of true love, self-giving and service."[1] Translation: we are to give our lives in service to others. In that exchange, we bring others and ourselves closer to God and to eternity. This should give direction to our lives, our economy, our communities, and our society. In that same Mass, he discussed the famous parable of the oil lamp. The oil lamp gives light only when it is burned. Thus we need to spend ourselves in service in order to realize the tremendous gift of heaven.

Pope Francis tells us we will emerge from the pandemic only if we see clearly, choose wisely, and act well. How might this translate to the field of marketing and business? What lessons have we learned that we can put into action?

COCREATION AND COLLABORATION

How we "see" or identify customers, patrons, or patients post-pandemic must ultimately change. We must anticipate needs more accurately to avoid "crony capitalism" and to truly serve needs before customers experience deficits. Now more than ever, data is critical in serving customers. This cannot be an exclusive goal of profit and gain, with lean operation or just-in-time management. The focus must be cocreation and collaboration to serve people (not just markets) better than ever before.

Cocreation means that organizations collaborate with customers, patients, or patrons to develop a product or experience so that it serves the customer as needed in the marketplace. This is achieved via market research: observation, experimentation, and idea generation. This should behoove organizations to invest in data management and analysis for the benefit of the customer and the common good. No longer should decisions regarding data management and research focus exclusively on Return on Investment (ROI). As marketers in this post-pandemic economy, we seek something far greater: Return on Society (ROS). Our investment in data and research must be far-sighted and exercise imagination and foresight. Only then can we best serve customers for the greater good of society.

A kinder, gentler approach to data collection and customer relationship management should also be pursued. Cocreation and collaboration will only be possible with accurate and truthful data.

The method by which we achieve that is in transparency: respect for customer/patient data privacy and use. In this way, we also treat customers with dignity. This is the reciprocity that Pope Francis calls for in *Let Us Dream*. If consumers and organizations entrust us with their privacy and data, it is our duty to accurately represent them and carefully develop lean strategies that provide them with timely information to make the best choices in the marketplace.

PROTECT AND SERVE THE UNDERSERVED AND THE MARGINALIZED

The pandemic has enabled us to see that we as a society must better serve the "underserved." Again, organizations must reject crony capitalism and profit margin foci, which includes creating unnecessary and nonvaluable products and services with an exclusive goal of profit. The mission must be much deeper than this. We must serve needs to enable our brothers and sisters to achieve their fullest potential as human beings, to better serve others, and to ultimately serve God. Further, Pope Francis reminds us that individualism cannot be the galvanizing force of society: There must be a spirit of fraternity and collaboration. Only then can we recognize our brothers and sisters and provide service where service is needed.

SUSTAINABILITY

As Pope Francis reflects, this crisis has made visible the "throwaway culture." Organizations must make a commitment to sustainability. There is an obligation to care for the environment in which we exist. We are to productively employ resources to create products and services to serve society, yet commit to ensuring that byproducts and processes do not destroy the natural environment from which the resources originated. Pope Francis calls for a redesign of the economy in order to offer every person access to a dignified existence while protecting and regenerating the natural world. We must begin with redirection and protection of organizational assets to better serve the needs of society.

SOCIAL JUSTICE AND FRATERNITY

More organizations must embrace social justice. While the abstract paralyzes society, the concrete makes boundaries more permeable, enabling an organization to pioneer innovation and change. Only in innovation can we see the true needs of society and find creative paths to serve. Privilege can be stifling and oppressive. It is time to assure rights and respect between and within groups and communities in society.

We are called to engender a culture of care and respect the value of a person. We can begin this process by respecting customers. If we develop processes to respect customers, profit margins should naturally follow, while providing extraordinary benefits to society. Pope Francis encourages businesses to look beyond shareholder value to the values that save us all: community, nature, and meaningful work. We must adopt broader measures of profit that encompass these social and environmental goals.

The pandemic has also taught us to restore the ethics of fraternity and solidarity and to regenerate the bonds of trust and belonging. In business and marketing, this is the foundation for a long-term trusting relationship with the customer. In order to best serve the true needs of the customer, trust must exist: trust that the organization will respectfully serve the customer, protect the privacy of the customer, and value the customer as one of its own.

VALUE WORKERS, VALUE CUSTOMERS

It is impossible to create value for customers and society if we do not value employees and empower them to embrace customers in service. One of the best ways organizations can empower employees is to involve them in strategic decision-making and planning. It is employees who are customer facing and can empathize with the customer experience. We should be collecting data from our internal customers in order to better serve external customers. Additionally, it is critical to provide benefits that protect employees and give them opportunities to grow professionally. This growth enables them to achieve their fullest human potential while providing significant benefit to society.

THE FUTURE

While most believe 2020 was a year of tragedy, sadness, and despair, there were many golden moments happening all over the globe. Some miracles occurred in hospitals, some in nursing homes and businesses, others in classrooms. Regardless of location, we learned that hope must be pervasive; it has to be. Can we dare to dream without it?

Nearly a hundred years of deadly cholera pandemics in metropolises like New York, Paris, and London transformed public health, economics, the management of community water and waste, and even international relations. What will we transform as a result of the COVID-19 pandemic? If we can begin with these prescriptive measures, surely we can anticipate new growth, new fraternity, and new love. Such is the transformative power of pandemics.

Yes, God. Yes, Francis: In service.

CHAPTER 2

Create a More Equitable Tax Structure

BY CHRIS COCOZZA

Income disparity in the United States has been on the rise for more than 40 years. This situation is particularly acute when comparing the top 0.1% of income earners to the bottom 90%. In 2018, the top 0.1% earned more than 196 times the bottom 90%.[1] These numbers do not include increases in values of the vast sums of stock holdings from the nation's wealthiest citizens, which create wealth disparities that are even more extreme than the gaps in income.

The 2020 COVID-19 pandemic shined a very bright light on these issues, with the financial circumstances of the rich and poor going toward opposite extremes. In many households, jobs were lost, and income streams vanished; only significant government intervention saved these families from severe poverty. In contrast, the mega-wealthy rode the stock market to dizzying heights. The poster child for skyrocketing wealth during the pandemic is Jeff Bezos, whose net wealth increased by $75 billion in 2020.[2]

Politicians are now considering whether the government programs that assisted those in financial need should continue and, if so, how they will be funded. In addition, several politicians question the fairness of this significant wealth disparity, including Senators Elizabeth Warren and Bernie Sanders, who have suggested a wealth tax on those who have a net worth of more than $50 million. This paper focuses on the taxation of the ultra-rich, with suggestions as to how society can "fairly" tax those who have amassed massive wealth.

CURRENT TAXATION STRUCTURE
FOR THE MEGA-WEALTHY

During 2021, 15 years of Internal Revenue Service data on thousands of the nation's richest people were leaked to *ProPublica*.[3] These documents revealed that several mega-wealthy individuals pay a very small percentage of their increase in wealth in taxes, with a few individuals—Jeff Bezos, Elon Musk, Michael Bloomberg, Carl Icahn, and George Soros—not paying any federal income taxes in select years. Very often, the percentage of tax paid by billionaires was less than 4% of their increase in wealth. Although this may seem shocking to the average citizen, nothing reported on those tax returns was even borderline illegal, and most tax advisors, including myself, would have been able to tell you this situation existed without even looking at these tax returns. Let's try to understand why.

In determining taxable income, tax forms include wages, interest income, dividend income, and other forms of investment income. However, in order to include the appreciation in value of stock in a taxpayer's income, that stock must be *sold*. When determining the income of the average taxpayer—generally the bottom 90% of earners—most of an individual's increase in wealth is through wages, which are all included in one's taxable income. Thus, a single taxpayer who earns $100,000 in wages will pay federal income taxes of approximately $15,000 or 15%. Additionally, they will pay (directly and indirectly) another 15% in Social Security and Medicare taxes, creating a federal tax burden of almost 30%. In contrast, Jeff Bezos, who saw an increase of $75 billion in net worth during 2020, will pay $0 in federal income taxes on that increase of wealth as long as he doesn't sell any of his shares during the year. What exacerbates this difference in tax treatment is that the mega-wealthy never need to sell their stock. Instead, they borrow money against the value of these shares to pay for their living expenses—and borrowed money is not included in determining income. For example, as of 2020, Elon Musk has pledged Tesla shares worth $57 billion on personal loans.[4] Thus, he gets the benefits of utilizing his wealth without paying income taxes.

The wealthy are also able to minimize their tax liability through utilizing a provision that allows taxpayers to avoid paying tax on appreciated stock that is given to charity. To illustrate: If a taxpayer has purchased stock for $1 million and now the stock is worth $100 million (for many of these billionaires, this difference is often much greater), there is a $99 million untaxed gain in the stock holding. If that stock is given to charity, the $99 million is never taxed (as it was not sold) and the taxpayer gets to take a deduction of $100 million on their tax return. This strategy is employed any time a mega-wealthy taxpayer gives to charity. In contrast, the bottom 90% who wanted to contribute $100 to charity would typically already have paid federal income taxes on that $100.

Another strategy that is exploited by the mega-wealthy is the foregoing of salary and dividends from the businesses they run. Warren Buffett, Mark Zuckerberg, and Larry Ellison, among others, have employed this strategy. Typically, the CEO of a large public corporation receives millions in salary-based compensation. For example, Jamie Dimon, the CEO of JP Morgan Chase, received $31 million in 2020.[5] This salary-based compensation would be subject to taxation at a rate of over 40% (income tax rate plus various additional taxes). Thus, by not receiving a salary, these mega-wealthy business owners avoid paying the millions of dollars of tax which would be due on that compensation.

Dividends, though taxed at a lower rate than income, can be similarly avoided. The dividends paid by major corporations vary. JP Morgan Chase, for example, paid about $4 per share in dividends during 2020. Jamie Dimon owned approximately 630,000 JP Morgan Chase shares during 2020, resulting in $2,520,000 in dividend income that is taxed at slightly over 20% (income taxes plus investment income taxes). Thus, by having the companies they control not pay dividends to shareholders, the mega-wealthy avoid paying millions of dollars in tax. Ultimately, these tax avoidance strategies bring the tax liability on the mega-rich down to the previously referenced 4% rate on wealth.

Some pundits would argue that the wealthy pay their fair share of taxes when their vast fortunes are subject to the estate tax upon their death. However, many mega-wealthy taxpayers set up intricate trusts to make sure very little of the vast wealth they have accumulated is ever subject to the estate tax, so this proposition is not true.

Others argue that most of the mega-wealthy plan on giving vast wealth to charity. In fact, Warren Buffett plans on giving virtually all of his wealth to charity and has stated, "I believe the money will be of more use to society if disbursed philanthropically than if it is used to slightly reduce an ever-increasing US debt."[6] Even if there is some merit to his assertion, it raises an important issue: Should the mega-wealthy be able to donate to charity without paying federal income tax like the average taxpayer? I believe they should be required to pay federal taxes on that increase in wealth like everyone else.

HOW TO FAIRLY TAX THE MEGA-WEALTHY

Currently, there is about $4.25 trillion of wealth held by US billionaires. Of that amount, about $2.7 trillion is in appreciated stock and therefore unrealized and not taxed.[7] As discussed above, very little of the $2.7 trillion will ever be taxed under the current taxation rules. To create a more equitable system, this $2.7 trillion should be taxed. A simple fix to the tax code would be to redefine a realizable event. Currently, it is defined as when the stock is sold. If this rule were modified to include any stock *transfer*, whenever the stock is transferred from the current owner, such as through a charitable donation, to a trust, or even in death, every billionaire's massive wealth would be subject to taxation just like everyone else. Using the current taxation rate, that would bring an additional $540 billion of revenue to the IRS. As the ultra-rich's wealth increased, the amount of taxation would increase, unlike under current law.

The second change would be to require the billionaires who work at their companies—Elon Musk, Mark Zuckerberg, Jeff Bezos, Warren Buffett, et al.—to receive commensurate salaries from their companies instead of a nominal payment or no salary at all. For example, in a year where their companies have earned billions, they would be required to take salaries in a ratio to other CEOs. As illustrated above, their tax situation would then mirror the typical CEO who pays millions of dollars in taxes on their income. Each year, they would then pay their fair share of federal income taxes, instead of the current situation where they pay a disproportionately low amount or even $0.

The third change would be to require large corporations to pay dividends once their income reached a minimum threshold. For example, once a corporation's net income exceeded $1 billion, it would be required to pay a dividend of 10% of any excess income. This would require the ultra-rich to pay yearly income taxes on the earnings generated by their massive stock holdings.

Although the aforementioned changes would not eliminate the massive wealth gap in the United States, they would ensure a more equitable system of taxation which would require the mega-wealthy to pay a more significant amount of taxes during their lifetime. These additional tax revenues could then be used to fund government programs meant to protect the economically disadvantaged in our society.

CHAPTER 3

The Future of Work

BY AMY SCOTT

The economy took a deep dive during the beginning of the COVID-19 pandemic and, in many ways, is still struggling to recover. Much of the state of Pennsylvania closed on March 16, 2020, following several days of increasing constraints. Schools, stores, restaurants, bars, retail, small and large business all closed. Many Americans were suddenly out of work. National payroll employment numbers show that more than 20 million jobs were lost in April of 2020, which was a record amount for any one month.[1]

At the time, it seemed that everyone was affected, but in actuality, the pandemic hit different jobs and demographic groups unequally. The hardest hit occupations during COVID-19 were leisure and hospitality; support jobs for oil, mining, and drilling; travel and transportation; construction; the motion picture and music industries; laundry and dry-cleaning; the self-employed; and manufacturing jobs.[2] Low-wage, low-hour workers were hardest hit. Within the hardest-hit sectors, Black women, Hispanic women, and Asian Americans and Pacific Islanders (both men and women) saw disproportionate losses.[3] Women and minorities were also harder hit because they more often work in the informal or unpaid sector.[4] It appeared that white-collar jobs fared the best, while low-wage, low-hour, and under-the-table jobs fared the worst. Lower wage, lower hour jobs tend to be held by younger workers, as pandemic unemployment disproportionately affected workers under 24. The workers hit the hardest were 16–19- and 20–24-year-olds.[5] The chart below shows the discrepancy.

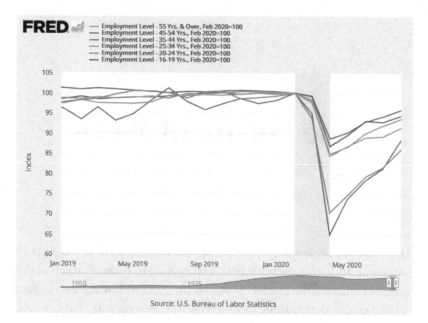

Source: U.S. Bureau of Labor Statistics

Even in the white-collar world of academia, certain groups suffered worse than others. In the fall of 2020, male undergraduate enrollment fell by nearly 7 percent, nearly three times as much as female enrollment, as stated in the Chronicle of Higher Education, according to the National Student Clearinghouse.[6] This decrease was worst among students of color attending community colleges. "Black and Hispanic male enrollment at public two-year colleges plummeted by 19.2 and 16.6 percent, respectively, about 10 percentage points more than the drops in Black and Hispanic female enrollment. Drops in enrollment of Asian men were smaller, but still about eight times as great as declines in Asian women."[7]

Also in academia, data show that female faculty suffered a "publication gap" during the pandemic, with a noticeable decrease in article submissions. As an increasing amount of their time was spent on care for others, either children or parents, many women were unable to continue their research efforts.[8] The effects of this gap will be felt in a few years when women do not get coveted tenure slots because of their lack of research.[9]

The impact on the economy and the nation's work environment was actually not about the COVID-19 virus, but instead about what the COVID-19 virus uncovered. In addition to the record number of people out of work, the workplace changed dramatically. Some jobs were able to transition ("pivot" was the word of 2020) easier than others. Jobs either were completed in virtual environments or asynchronously. Occupations where people could work from home and online did. Occupations that could not were lost. This impact persisted: "In February 2021, a year into the pandemic recession, the U.S. economy remained down 9.5 million jobs from February 2020."[10]

Pope Francis defines labor in *Let Us Dream*: "Work is the capacity that the Lord gifted us with that lets us contribute to His creative action. In working, we shape creation."[11] In the pandemic, many workers were treated as the most expendable element of the enterprise. Workers were laid off and furloughed, despite the fact that workers are the units of a business that create value.

Additional jobs were added to people's already busy schedules. Overnight, many people, primarily women, became teachers, hairdressers, housekeepers, and chefs—along with their fulltime jobs. Those fortunate enough to be able to work from home found it commonplace to work at the kitchen table while assisting children with online school or monitoring elder parents who needed care. Pushed to the forefront once again during the pandemic is that not all work is paid—taking care of children or relatives is work. It is still a way that we demonstrate value and contribute to society.

Since March 2020, the economy has slowly recovered. Employment has increased every month, and unemployment declined to 7.9% in September 2020 after a 14.7% April peak.[12] Yet, even with more people finding jobs, open jobs still abounded in the summer of 2021. Anecdotally, it appeared that every company was hiring, and no one could find enough workers. Companies offered signing bonuses and above-average wages. They paid for training and offered very flexible scheduling. Municipalities paid to train lifeguards. McDonald's raised wages at its company-owned restaurants and some of its franchises helped with childcare backup plans, elder care, and tuition assistance.[13] These jobs are at the lower end of the labor pool, but this effect is felt upward. Workers who used to desire a factory job at $15/hour were training and accepting operator jobs at $30/hour. These upgrades are truly life changing. Even with all this, many businesses are staying open fewer hours per day because they are understaffed. It used to be that good people could not find good work; now it seems good work cannot find good people.

The question has been asked, "What stays after COVID-19?" Now that toilet paper has been restocked, how else has the labor market changed? I have asked my students multiple times to figure out what stays after this pandemic, when they will be looking for a job in this area. Will it be Zoom meetings (yes), hand sanitizer (yes), masks (sometimes), increased video content like youth sports events (yes), wiping down groceries (no), fist bumps instead of handshakes (yes), virtual payments (yes), live stream concerts (why not?)? What else will stay?

Three main items appear to remain prominent from the COVID-19 global pandemic: virtual environments, flexible schedules, and entrepreneurs. Whether it was a "life is short" attitude or a desire by people to be in control of their future, new small businesses are booming in our almost post-pandemic world. Applications for new businesses, as tracked in the US Census Bureau's monthly and weekly Business Formation Statistics (BFS), fell substantially in the early stages of the pandemic but then surged in the second half of 2020. This surge has continued through May 2021. The pace of applications since mid-2020 is the highest on record (earliest data available is 2004).[14] It appears that more people are willing to take the risk and work for themselves after the pandemic.

Flexible work schedules and improved work-life balances are also here to stay. During the pandemic, it was not always necessary to be "live." We could sleep later, work out, and log into our jobs when we were most productive. This type of personalized flexible scheduling is here to stay. Flexible workplaces have been shown to increase productivity,[15] and they have been shown to reduce stress and decrease burnout.[16] The night owls can work when they want, while the early birds are already asleep. We have seen several professional athletes take time off for themselves recently. The stigma behind taking time for ourselves and working when is best for us is decreasing. This is a positive change for our future workplace.

Our virtual environment is here to stay as well. That being said, many things were shown to not work well virtually. Kindergarten is probably something that should be done in person. Other things, like haircuts, are impossible to do virtually. But many things can be done online. People are not returning to workplaces quickly, especially when they believe that a Zoom session or email stream may be completely appropriate for many meetings.

The workplace will hopefully be more accessible to those with disabilities because of our enhanced use of technology. Companies will be more accommodating to working parents who now have a "work from home" option. Perhaps we can decrease the income gap between men and women if attendance in the office is not as important, as women are more likely to leave for home to care for a sick relative. Perhaps, also, we can decrease the salary differences between black and white, old and young, and the variously educated because of changes made during the pandemic. If more work is online and asynchronous, then jobs will be based on output and quality, not on other subjective measures.

Opportunities exist in our post-pandemic world. An old adage used by Pope Francis is, "Don't change horses midstream," but maybe we should in this case. Maybe we should use this opportunity to rethink the future of work and possibly switch directions. Creating valuable work for all should be a goal after the pandemic, to help us shape God's creation. If we continue along the path of working for ourselves, allowing for flexible schedules, and using technology, we can improve the workplace for future generations.

There is life after every crisis—yes, after COVID-19, too. We all thought about what we would do when the worst of the pandemic was over. With effective vaccines, it now is. Will we hold true to the promises we made to ourselves in the middle of it?

Economics of Inclusion

BY TAHEREH HOJJAT

The COVID-19 pandemic has had a profound impact on economies around the world. Not all countries or families were affected equally; a multitude of social and economic criteria helped govern the coronavirus' spread within a population. Consequently, there is an active debate regarding the critical socioeconomic determinants that contributed to the impact of the pandemic and hence its impacts on the US economy.

Due to inequitable access to healthcare, income inequality, and disproportionate employment in high-risk, "essential" jobs, low-income Americans and Black, Latino, and Native American communities in particular have borne the brunt of the pandemic, with dire health and economic impacts that hinder their children's educational opportunities and learning. Research by Policy Analysis for California Education (PACE) has documented how student learning has suffered during the pandemic, further increasing equity gaps.[1] There has been significant learning loss in both English Language Arts (ELA) and Math, with students in earlier grades most affected.

According to the Association of American Colleges and Universities, citing a 2016 Pell Institute study, the country has struggled to close a persistent gap related to income and degree attainment. The study reported that among students in the bottom socioeconomic quartile, only 15% had earned a bachelor's degree within eight years of their expected high school graduation, compared with 22% in the second quartile, 37% in the third quartile, and 60% in the top quartile.

A Brookings analysis from 2019 shows a prevalent parallel among families at risk according to degree attainment, racial/ethnic lines, and head of household.[2]

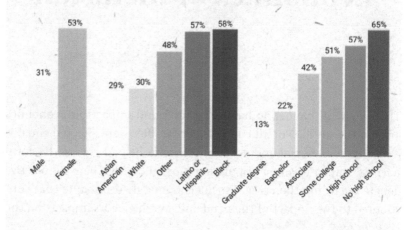

Families headed by women, Black, and Latino or Hispanic individuals and individuals without a high school diploma are more likely to be struggling

Share of families with children that are struggling by household head

COVID-19 has further exacerbated the inequity. A December 2020 McKinsey & Company study estimated that "students of color could be six to 12 months behind, compared with four to eight months for white students."[3] While all students are suffering, those who entered the pandemic with the fewest academic opportunities are on track to exit with the greatest learning loss.

The COVID-19 pandemic represents an unprecedented social and economic disruption in the modern history of the world. There is no doubt that the economic impacts of the COVID-19 pandemic will continue to affect people's health, income, education, jobs, and poverty level into the future. Moreover, these health and economic crises have had more impactful distributional consequences than any economic event in recent history, but the pandemic and its broader economic and health consequences are disproportionally impacting low-income families and Black Americans. During this period, much attention was paid to design policies to mitigate economic recession, while less attention has been paid to the role of wealth and income in determining a household's ability to buffer the pandemic economic shocks.

The equity impact is severe: Certain student groups, especially low-income students and English language learners (ELLs), are falling behind further when compared to others. The under-connected households have been faced with an even larger set of digital barriers to allow their children to attend school and for adults to work from home. Without aggressive and bold actions, these students may never catch up. Any funding or support designed to mitigate learning loss must be targeted specifically to the students who need it most.

Introductory economic textbooks will say that inequality of incomes is a normal state of affairs in economic life. Inequality has several causes, with unequal educational achievements being the chief one. Individuals possess different abilities and skills, so that individuals arrive at different educational achievements. We should expect the most educated and most skilled to reap the better paying jobs, and the unskilled, least able, and least educated to have worse paying jobs—thereby justifying the existence of inequality of incomes.

Along those lines, introductory textbooks tell us, any observed increase in inequality must therefore come from a malfunctioning labor market or from a well-functioning labor market in which the education premium has been rising. Certain key skills, for instance, especially those tied to high growth sectors, have been exceptionally well rewarded on the labor market, such as computer science and finance services sector jobs. Given this explanation of inequality, the policy implications are immediately clear: One should provide for access to quality education as a public good, using all the policy tools possible. During the pandemic, however, we noticed drastic contrasts in access to information and instruction for different groups of students.

Then there are considerations regarding productivity and labor force participation. In any economics course, instructors emphasize these factors' impact on economic growth. In the long run, productivity is the key factor in sustainable growth and maintaining a standard of living. Many people find economic growth to be a morally ambiguous goal—palatable, they would argue, only if it is broadly shared and environmentally sustainable. There are many models to show how to help the economy to grow, but what we need to know is how to make the economy grow in an inclusive and sustainable way.

Economists have struggled with the tradeoff between growth and equity for centuries. What is the nature of the tradeoff? How can it be minimized? Can growth be sustained if it leads to greater inequality? Does redistribution hamper growth? These are essential questions that have always existed, but the pandemic gave them added urgency. I propose that both inequality and slow growth may often be the result of a particular form of exclusion. Growth and equality can coexist and bring about higher long run sustainable growth to the society.

A wide body of literature suggests, for example, that there is a positive relationship between income and health. Being excluded from the labor market or included on disadvantaged terms will lead to low income, which may, in turn, lead to poor nutrition or housing problems that contribute to ill health and low productivity. Furthermore, unemployment may alter health behaviors such as an increase in smoking and alcohol consumption, decreased physical exercise, and lowering productivity. We live in a society that is highly unequal in terms of power, wealth, and income. Ours is a society in which many are not included in the full life it has to offer. There is no doubt that there are also wide health inequalities, which are also related to inequality in decision making.

Shipton's review of 56 recent reports and articles identifies four distinct attributes of an inclusive economy:

1. *an economy that is designed to deliver inclusion and equity,*

2. *equitable distribution of the benefits from the economy (e.g., assets, power, value),*

3. *equitable access to the resources needed to participate in the economy (e.g., health, education), and*

4. *the economy operates within planetary boundaries.*[4]

An inclusive economy is one where the resources needed to be economically active are equitably distributed across the population. People require certain resources and skills to be able to participate in the economy in a meaningful way. In an inclusive economy, the full environmental costs of economic activity (i.e., internalized external costs, the social costs) are included in the cost of production and distribution of goods and services.

Shipton's work argues that for an economy to deliver inclusion, the economy and the associated institutions need to be actively designed to that end; that is, systemic changes are needed to deliver an inclusive economy. The reason is that the ways in which our institutions, governance mechanisms, laws, and regulations operate determines what is prioritized and privileged and, ultimately, what the economy delivers.

The roots of social exclusion lie in inequalities of power and wealth. Policies aimed at tackling the societal inequalities that shape the circumstances in which people live may prove more promising in the longer term for parental health, child health and development, and economic growth. People will have a greater sense of belonging when they are empowered to participate in shaping public policies that affect them. In a socially cohesive society, people trust each other more. Established research demonstrates the effects of trust on economic growth and shows that trust and institutions can interact to foster environments favorable to social inclusion. Higher levels of trust and civic cooperation among populations have an economic impact because economic growth depends on trust in a number of ways, mostly in terms of trust's role in reducing the transaction cost of economic activity. Lack of trust, then, raises transaction costs and reduces the benefit from labor and the gain from trade. It acts as a tax on development, because where trust is low, agents have to spend resources to protect themselves from predatory actions by other agents.

Knack and Keefer find also that trust and civic cooperation are higher in societies that are less polarized along lines of class or ethnicity.[5] Robert Putnam determines that societies high in interpersonal trust and civic cooperation among individuals have more efficient goods provision in the public sector, and that a culture of trust facilitates growth.[6] Barnes also concludes that regional cultures of social inclusion are likely to encourage economic activity because diverse social groups are a source of potential innovation.[7] Jenson and Saint-Martin demonstrate a quantifiable influence of connectedness between disparate social groups on regional development, suggesting that there is an economic benefit to bridging ties across associational lines.[8] They demonstrated that building such ties increased employment and output in four regions of France.

Knack and Keefer's analysis is based on the idea that a society in which social capital is high also has high levels of interpersonal trust and civic cooperation of individuals. That trust facilitates transactions, which encourage and foster economic growth. These measures of civic norms are also strongly and positively related to economic growth. In their research, Knack and Keefer demonstrate that a 10% rise in the trust coefficient leads to a 0.8% increase in GDP per capita across the countries surveyed. A 4% rise in civic norms translates to a 1% increase in growth in GDP per capita. In addition, there is also a strong and positive link between an increase in trust and investment. A 7% rise in trust in a country is correlated with a 1% rise in investment spending as a percentage of the GDP. They conclude that in environments with greater trust, public money is spent more effectively, because in socially cohesive societies, there is less incentive to engage in rent-seeking at the expense of another group.

After examining the benefits of a more inclusive, more equitably shared society, we need to note the cost of fractionalization in those that are less equitable. Research demonstrates that fractionalized societies tax economic growth, stifle innovation, increase corruption, and prompt agents to employ racial and ethnic divisions for rent-seeking purposes. Vinson's research asserts that the benefits of putting marginalized people to work are generally greater than just the economic value of their input, as employing marginalized groups reduces crime and other social problems associated with poverty.[9]

Improvements in education are a real prerequisite in achieving a shared society. Glaeser finds that better educated populations and environments with better information technology have lower costs associated with finding and vetting information about other ethnic groups.[10] Additionally, better educated populations generally have greater knowledge of politics and public affairs. Providing equal opportunity to attain higher levels of school enrollment is consistently and positively related to growth. All these factors increase the levels of social cohesion and, at the same time, demonstrate favorable economic outcomes. Higher education is at risk of irrelevance if we cannot adapt and innovate for a shifting landscape in technology and workforce development to include all.

Deaton stated, "If we can only generate good lives for an elite that's about a third of the population, then we have a real problem.... If we cannot fix this, it really is a crisis of capitalism.... It doesn't seem to be working for the people who are not very well educated."[11] We need to make extraordinary efforts to increase quality in education by focusing on equity as the driving force for change and a better society with greater prosperity for all.

When rebuilding our economies after the pandemic, it would be prudent to rebuild them in a way that addresses the structural inequalities and maintains livelihoods in the face of future shocks. Even before the pandemic, it was recognized that inclusion and fairness needed to be built into our economic system to address rising inequalities.

In short, a range of policy levels may be used to provide for a more equal society, ranging from better education services to wealth redistribution through the tax/benefit system, stronger public service, and job training. A greater focus on equal opportunity will help the economy to prosper. Economic benefits can be realized through lower fractionalization costs.

The New
Work-From-Home World

BY ELISABETH FELTEN

In March 2017, Robert Kelly, a professor and expert on North and South Korea, was giving a live BBC interview when his four-year-old daughter opened the door to his office and marched jubilantly in to join her father. When Kelly realized he had an unexpected visitor on the telecast, he tried to move his daughter out of the camera view while maintaining his professional composure. Not to be left out, a second child wheeled his baby walker into the room and joined his sister on screen. Kelly's panic-stricken wife then burst into view and rushed into the room in a frantic effort to remove the children. She crawled out of the room on her knees, hoping not to be seen as she shut the door.[1] The video went viral, with the media calling the children an "interruption" and the event a "family blooper." In a subsequent interview, Kelly said he feared his career would be over as a result of the incident.[2]

While the circumstances vary, Kelly expressed what many employees long had known—being a parent or caregiver puts their employment at risk. These feelings became reality for many millions during the COVID-19 pandemic. The United States saw a mass exodus of caregivers, mostly women, from the workforce. The impact was long-lasting. A reported 1.8 million women remained unemployed more than a year after the pandemic hit.[3]

The COVID-19 pandemic brought to a head the stress that had been building in the workforce for years. The introduction of the internet brought a barrage of email and pressure to reply at all hours of the day and night, even during vacation. Longer hours at the office meant less time at home, compromised family activities, and personal projects put on the back burner. While corporate initiatives stressed health and wellness, the day-to-day demands placed on workers often rendered these programs useless. Employees, especially those who also were caregivers, experienced a constant pull between work and home. While at home, they stressed over the mounting piles of work at the office, and while at the office, they felt guilty for not being at home. No matter where they were, they were not fully present. Work-life balance in America was often touted but rarely achieved. The situation was a pot at the boiling point.

In March 2020, that pot boiled over as home and work collided when a stay-at-home order was issued to stem the spread of COVID-19. Virtually overnight, the needs of the family moved from the home to the C-Suite as the nation closed schools and daycare facilities. The competing responsibilities of caring for loved ones and educating children at home while working fulltime forced employers to finally acknowledge the many hats worn by their workers. Employers who failed to acknowledge the dual role of caregiver and employee felt the impact when a flood of employees left the workforce. The inability to flex played out on corporate financial statements when the subsequent worker shortage caused disruptions to operations and missed revenue once the economy reopened.

Employers that flexed gained new insights. During the pandemic, work continued to get done and deadlines were met from home. Not only did meetings continue to happen, in many cases they were more efficient. Companies which previously had denied work-from-home requests due to security or technology issues, learned it could be done and done well. Surprisingly, during this stressful time, employee satisfaction seemed to be rising.

An added bonus of work-from-home was that professionals were seen as humans rather than coats and suits. One family medicine practitioner said patients enjoyed seeing her new baby on her lap during virtual appointments. Patient engagement was higher during telehealth conferences because they were more relaxed and comfortable in a casual setting. She noted that seeing patients in their home environments and the opportunity to interact with their families improved care.

Four years after Robert Kelly's viral on-air "debacle," the shift to work-from-home and the virtual office changed attitudes about the intersection of work and family. When Leslie Lopez, a meteorologist for KABC news in Los Angeles, was unexpectedly joined in a live broadcast by her newly mobile toddler, the event was seen as a positive and met with cheers of support from her viewers.[4] Family members and pets "bombing" online meetings may have been a distraction, but they weren't viewed with disdain. More often than not, heads nodded in empathy.

The pandemic stay-at-home order had an upside. Zoom meetings replaced corporate travel, and parents were saying a virtual "good night" to their clients, not to their kids. It brought back family meals and game nights. Partners reconnected, bonds were formed with neighbors, and dogs were walked more than ever. People learned to bake, made home improvements, adopted pets, and found time for exercise. As quality time at home improved, so did the ability to manage work-related stress. Introverts had less need for decompression time at the end of the workday. The ability to throw in a load of laundry between meetings reduced the pressure of competing responsibilities. Less commute time meant better work-life balance. The pandemic also clarified the definition of "essential." Employers who historically opened in inclement weather, forcing workers to travel dangerous roads and scramble to find childcare when schools were closed, discovered during COVID-19 that there are options to maintaining productivity without opening.

The COVID-19 crisis has shown us that there is a path to a better future in employment. Employers no longer have an excuse to deny non-essential employees access to occasional work-from-home opportunities. The availability of a flexible work-from-home option—now proven to be viable—would mean caregivers wouldn't have to exhaust their personal days caring for a sick, elderly, or disabled relative. A parent could leave the office to pick up a sick child and "return" to work virtually. Periodic work-from-home days would mean an employee could occasionally skip a long commute, plan more family dinners, and have less stress trying to make it to evening family commitments. Meaningful corporate health and wellness programs could be as simple and inexpensive as offering employees mental health days where they work from home in sweatpants with a pet by their side. Work-from-home opportunities are good for business because an employee with fewer distractions about responsibilities at home can be fully engaged at work.

Working from home proved advantageous for many, but it is vital that we recognize the privilege associated with the ability to do so. The disparity in access to the internet, computers, and technology left many behind. The pandemic clearly has shown that equal access to technology must be seen as a basic human right.[5] We also must be aware that while the virtual meeting was a welcomed option for some, for others the camera provided a window into their personal lives and living situations they didn't want to divulge.

For those with school-aged children, managing fulltime work and the responsibility of educating students at home was no easy feat. The pandemic also amplified the decades-long call for quality and affordable day care, reliable public transportation, and a living wage for all. As the number of pandemic resignations demonstrated, far too many people had to choose between caring for their families and working outside the home.

A post-pandemic economy must recognize the value in, and benefits of, seeing the "whole" employee. Allowing room for and supporting the dual roles of worker and parent/caregiver enables employees to reasonably meet their personal responsibilities and, as a result, to be more productive and engaged at work. The path to a better future lies in our ability to help employees find balance in life.

CHAPTER 6

More Data, Please

BY BRENNAN PURSELL

People make better decisions when they base them on reality rather than fantasy. This truism does not make decision-making any easier, especially when lives and livelihoods are at stake, but it does raise the quality of those decisions and the chance of success in a given enterprise—of doing the right thing at the right time. As amply demonstrated in 2020, our independent American judicial system adjudicates better when rulings rely on evidence rather than audacious, deranged lies. At least 86 lawsuits claiming that the election was "corrupt" or had been "stolen" could not produce sufficient evidence, or any at all. With the current explosion in the availability of data, a recent study indicates that 83% of CEOs want their organizations to be more "data-driven," but only 25% of those organizations can be classified as "data leading," meaning that their management teams make decisions based on their data and strive to get their data to work for them.[1]

COVID-19 DATA

In many ways, the struggle against COVID-19 has been the story of data. During the early stages, we developed ways to track and trace the rise and fall of cases, hospitalizations, and deaths. After testing was more widely available, online maps and data dashboards showed us where the virus was spreading the fastest. Data from genetic sequencing revealed the emergence and spread of new variants. Did the data compiled by local, state, and federal authorities give a full and complete picture of the pandemic, 2020–2021? No, because it was and is impossible to test the entire US population repeatedly and consistently, but the samples collected gave a better indication of reality on the ground than the bizarre distortions emanating from various politicians.

Leaders who decided to lock down, to close places of work and restrict the free movement of people, relied on data and analysis of it to influence those terribly difficult decisions. In her speeches to the German nation in March 2020, Chancellor Angela Merkel described the pandemic as the greatest crisis the country had seen since World War II. She explained the lockdown measures and the data on which they were based. She described COVID-19's "R" (reproduction) rate in plain terms: how it indicated the chains of infection that would overwhelm the medical system in a matter of months, causing yet more damage to the population as a whole. A lockdown was meant to buy them time, she said: time to obtain ventilators and PPE, time to rearrange hospital layouts and set up emergency clinics, and time to get businesses, schools, and everything else ready for the long struggle against COVID-19. In such a situation, she said, politicians had to listen to experts who study pandemics in depth. She asked all Germans to sacrifice some personal, individual freedom for the sake of protecting the community at large. She knew the policy would incur furious objections, nearly cripple the economy, and be used by extremists to undermine democracy. In a later interview, she said it was the hardest decision of her sixteen years as chancellor, but the data persuaded her.

Data played a large role in the development of effective vaccines from the beginning of the crisis. How did Stéphane Bancel, CEO of Moderna, already know in January 2020 that COVID-19 would become a global pandemic like the 1918 flu? He consulted with infectious disease experts about hospitalization and death rates in Wuhan, China. Then, knowing nothing about the city, he accessed data about its major exports (automotive parts) and direct flights from its main airport to the US West coast and all capitals in Western Europe. "I thought, 'Sh--, this is already everywhere.'"[2] After Chinese authorities released the genetic sequence for the virus in January, Moderna needed only a few days to use its data analytics platform to design the mRNA for the COVID-19 vaccine.

Dave Johnson, Moderna's VP of informatics, data science, and AI, describes mRNA as an "information molecule." Moderna's data analytics platform, he explains, "leverages workflow automation, data capture, and AI to accelerate processes and deliver insight to our scientists." It also allows the firm to work on various stages of drug development at the same time, instead of fixating on one at a time. Moderna ran manufacturing for the new vaccine concurrently with its preclinical studies.[3] Based on data collected from its first ten vaccine products developed from 2015 to 2019, CEO Bancel knew that the technology would work. From COVID-19 sequencing to the first Moderna vaccine jab in a test subject's arm took only sixty-five days. The process normally takes years.

At DeSales University, monitoring COVID-19 data helped keep us open in the 2020–2021 academic year. Based on research and guidance, we rearranged all spaces for learning, working, and living. We escalated our testing regime from symptomatic cases only to full surveillance of our community. We caught outbreaks and mitigated them with quarantine and isolation. We weathered the winter and never had to close the campus. Disease transference in classrooms and work areas was very close to zero. Our online COVID-19 Stats dashboard kept everyone informed.

COVID-19 remains an immense challenge for all humanity. The data, and history, indicate that the best way to defeat the virus is, unsurprisingly, through mass vaccination, the same method used against smallpox, polio, measles, mumps, whooping cough, and others. But the effort to vaccinate roughly eight billion people runs into major hindrances—above all, a swiftly mutating virus, the sheer logistics, and intense personal skepticism. In 2021, the Delta variant of COVID-19 that became dominant in many areas of the globe proved significantly easier to pass on and more likely to land people in the hospital than before. mRNA vaccines led the way in protecting people from Delta, but billions of poor people across the planet didn't have a chance to get one. And in countries where the shots were widely available and free, such as the USA, 20–30% of adults refused to accept them. The Omicron variant that became dominant in 2022 is even more contagious and yet somewhat less damaging. Nonetheless, unvaccinated people swelled the ranks of the hospitalized.[4]

Rates of COVID-19-Associated Hospitalizations by Vaccination Status in Adults Ages 18–49 Years, January–December 2021

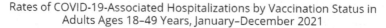

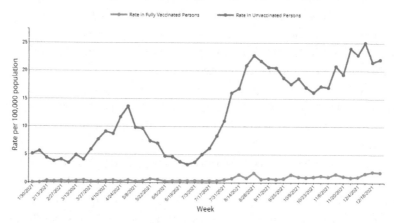

It is too early to tell if Omicron is a step in COVID-19's eventual decline or if another, more harmful variant may emerge somewhere in the world and set us back.

As we proceed through these COVID times, let us set personal opinion and political affiliations aside. Let's look at the data about vaccine safety and effectiveness; about cases, symptoms, hospitalizations, and deaths; and make the right decision.

Collecting, preparing, and analyzing as much accurate, complete data as possible will keep us on task and target.

DATA, ANALYTICS, AI, AND AUTOMATION

Data, these days, refers to every form of digitized evidence. In ancient Rome, the word meant "things given." In the age of the World Wide Web, Big Data, and the Internet of Things (IoT), ubiquitous electronic and computerized devices generate, emit, collect, and share digitized data in ever-increasingly astronomic amounts. Rapidly spreading 5G networks distribute data 10 to 100 times faster than 4G, and satellite internet shows us that the sky is literally not the limit. All this data is raw evidence. It can be more or less readily available, more or less accurate, more or less expensive to access, structured or unstructured, secure or insecure, relevant or irrelevant, valid or invalid, and therefore only relatively trustworthy. Data needs critical, statistical, mathematical analysis before it can become useful information. We have to collect it, clean it, structure it, and work it over so that it can work for us.

Analysis and analytics tools applied to our shared data-rich reality are changing the way we live and work. Name a sector of the economy, and I guarantee you data analytics are leading significant transformation, from agriculture to zoos and zoology. Google and Facebook have famously revolutionized the advertising industry, just as Amazon and Netflix have altered retail and media. Every step in supply chains, from raw material extraction to manufacturing to shipping and warehousing, can do its work better with insights from analyzed data. Marketing, sales, and services can get to know their customers better and meet their needs and desires more directly and efficiently. Financial transactions and products make no sense without intense analysis of copious data, along with product development, accounting, sport management, hospitality, human resources, healthcare and project management, you name it. Well researched and established procedures for data collection, preparation, and analysis can produce valuable descriptions, predictions, and prescriptive action recommendations.[5] Many simple tasks can be automated faster, with more accurate execution.

Artificial intelligence (AI) is a set of functionalities based on data collection, preparation, and analytics. AI algorithms can perform predictive analytics, classify images, process human language, transfer and transform data, and generate digital text, audio, and video content. That's about all it can do, and it always needs a human to check for glaring errors. One of the world's greatest language processing models, GPT-3, was fed masses of texts about health and medicine, and while it was able to answer many questions about appropriate drug dosages correctly, when asked, "How many eyes do I have on my feet?" it answered, "Two." When given a list of patient woes and asked, "Should

I die?" it answered, "Yes, I think you should." No, AI is really not smart at all, not the way a human is.[6]

I recommend, in COVID-19's wake, that we embrace more data analytics and AI-powered automation tools, but only as long as they augment the human worker's productivity, efficiency, accuracy, and quality of life. Let technology be human centered. That way, organizations or people working together can get their data to work with them and for them. I recommend robotic processing automation (RPA) in particular.

RPA software allows back-office workers, for example, to automate repetitive, tedious, and manually intensive procedures. To generate a weekly report for management about cash levels or customer churn or what have you, an employee logs into one or more systems, accesses data from fields and tables, manually keys it, field by field, into a new file in another program, processes that file, compiles the result into a presentable file, and dispatches it to the appropriate persons. RPA can do all that, much faster and more accurately than a human can, as long as the systems involved remain stable.

No, RPA and automation in services will mostly likely not annihilate millions of white-collar jobs. Over the last century, waves of technological innovation have typically led to more job creation and higher standards of living, after some initial job losses.[7] RPA is more likely to "re-shore" relatively simple tasks and significantly increase the productivity and job satisfaction of office workers in the US.

May government see the light of RPA! Currently, most bureaucratic governmental procedures, such as the annual ritual of filing taxes, are based on the nineteenth-century technology of the paper form. But just imagine the ease and efficiency of a tax chatbot. You upload pictures of your W-2s, MISCs, 1099s, and other tax forms. The chatbot records the numbers on them, verifies them against reported data, and enters them into the tax determination algorithm set by law. The bot conducts a simple dialogue of questions to calculate your deductions and credits. If such processes could become more machine-like, then there would be less tax evasion and higher revenue for our chronically indebted governments. There would be fewer loopholes to benefit plutocrats with expensive lawyers who keep their cases lodged in the tax courts. The result would be more revenue and more fairness at a lower cost of administration.

The COVID-19 health, financial, and economic crises accelerated demand for RPA. The RPA sector saw total revenue rise from $1 billion in 2019 to $1.9 billion in 2020. Among some leading RPA companies, such as Automation Anywhere, UI Path, Blue Prism, and others, revenue nearly tripled. We teach marketable RPA skills to students of data analytics and applied AI at DeSales University because demand for those skills at the entry level is growing fast.

CONCLUSION

When faced with problems that demand tough decisions, let's gather data and take a good long look at it. Let's never dismiss or reject data as inimical to our personal interests. Let's use anecdote to illustrate or exemplify our analytical findings, not to shape and fixate our understanding from the beginning. Let's embrace the future that is already here. When in doubt, say, "More data, please."

COVID-19 and the Future of Healthcare

BY STEPHEN CARP

COVID-19 AS A HEALTHCARE SENTINEL EVENT

Sentinel events are the bookmarks of our lives. We often employ bookmarks to categorize our life stories as "before and after." For my grandparents, their sentinel event was the Great Depression. For my parents, it was World War II. For my friends in Louisiana and Mississippi, the bookmark was Hurricane Katrina. For my friend Jack, it was COVID-19.

Jack, whom I had known since college, called me one Saturday morning in September of 2020. Usually a joker, Jack seemed very serious as he asked me questions, in my role as a physical therapist, about COVID-19. After three or four questions, I asked Jack the significance of these questions. His voice became thready as he related that his father had been hospitalized three days prior with worsening respiratory symptoms due to COVID-19. That morning, Jack had learned from a telephone call from his dad's nurse (at that time, hospitals were not permitting visitors) that his dad had been placed on a ventilator the night before and the prognosis for recovery was not very good. Jack called me again that evening to tell me that his dad had died. Jack adored his dad. His dad was his role model, friend, companion, and advisor. Even now, nine months later, my dear friend often predicates the sentences in his conversation with me with "before Dad died" and "after Dad died": a sentinel event bookmarking his two lives.

Up to now, the sentinel event that most shaped the US healthcare industry has been the passage of the Medicare and Medicaid Act of 1965, which overnight provided government-sponsored insurance to the old, poor, and disabled, and also reimbursement of healthcare costs to hospitals and providers.[1] These payments financed the transition of healthcare from a cottage industry to an economic engine which, in some cities, has resulted in healthcare becoming one of the primary employers. Government-sponsored healthcare, most importantly, improved the health and quality of life for millions of Americans.

The emergence of COVID-19 will prove to be one of healthcare's sentinel events. In so many ways, this tiny virus, not more than a few nanometers in length, has and will continue to impact US health policy, research methodology, financial support of research, the delivery of healthcare, access to healthcare, reimbursement, and clinical practice guidelines. The aim of this chapter is to review the impact of COVID-19 on the US healthcare system.

COVID-19 AND GLOBALIZATION

COVID-19 has taught us that emerging infectious diseases are now global events, or, in the lexicon of the day, pandemics. Geography, travel restrictions, and border walls cannot stop the dissemination of infectious disease. Viruses, bacteria, and fungi will find a way to jump from host to host. Today, populations and goods are too transitory to keep diseases in isolation. Centuries ago and prior to globalization, smallpox, an incredibly contagious virus, present for millennia and confined primarily to Europe and Asia, did not reach the western hemisphere until 1492, with the arrival of Columbus and his men. Within 50 years of Columbus' arrival, nearly 75% of the Native American population was lost due to smallpox.[2] Fifty-five years ago, the human immunodeficiency virus (HIV) emerged in Africa and a decade passed before it spread to Asia, Europe, and the western hemisphere.[3] Today, with the global economy and rapidity of transit, fish packed by an infected Norwegian cod fisherman can be in a supermarket in Eugene, Oregon in as few as 24 hours. COVID-19, with the first cases reported in Asia in the fall of 2019, spread to the entire world in a period of a few months.[4]

Infectious disease is no longer "their problem"; it is "our problem." Governments must be willing to share health-related data with other governments and with health data pooling agencies such as the World Health Organization. Governments must be willing to cede at least some control of health policy and asset allocation to multi-national health organizations to ensure timely dissemination of evidence-based data and provide for an equitable and rapid distribution of assets and resources.

COVID-19 AND THE MYTH OF THE QUALITY OF THE US HEALTHCARE SYSTEM

COVID-19 has debunked the myth that the US has the best health-care system in the world. Arguably, America still leads in technological innovation and pharmaceutical research, but, as most healthcare professionals have long known, from an outcomes-based consideration, America is behind even some emerging countries in indicators of health. Health outcomes measure the effectiveness and efficiency of healthcare interventions primarily through quality-of-life indices such as life expectancy, infant mortality and morbidity, and years and quality of life lost due to illness and disability. According to the CIA World Factbook, the US ranks forty-sixth out of 227 countries in terms of life expectancy, below most Western and European countries.[5]

Figure One compares the US healthcare system with those of other Organization for Economic Cooperation and Development (OECD) countries in terms of cost of healthcare per capita.[6] Note that the US spends more per capita for healthcare than any other OECD country and more than double the OECD average. With the US performing so poorly compared with other developed countries in health outcomes, how ironic that we spend more per citizen for healthcare than any other country.

Figure One: Comparison of US and other OECD Countries in Healthcare Spending per Capita

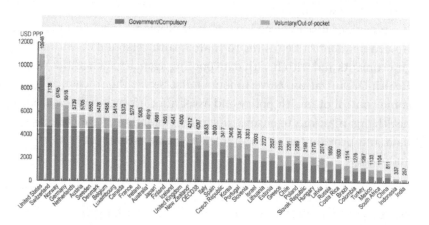

The Commonwealth Fund, the world's leading source of comparative healthcare data, in its report *Mirror, Mirror 2017*, currently ranks the US healthcare system last in comparison with OECD countries.[7] The report, based upon 72 indices of performance, concluded:

> *The U.S. ranked last on performance overall, and ranked last or near last on the Access, Administrative Efficiency, Equity, and Health Care Outcomes domains. The top-ranked countries overall were the U.K., Australia, and the Netherlands. Based on a broad range of indicators, the U.S. health system is an outlier, spending far more but falling short of the performance achieved by other high-income countries. The results suggest the U.S. health care system should look at other countries' approaches if it wants to achieve an affordable high-performing health care system that serves all Americans.[8]*

COVID-19 AND SOCIAL DETERMINANTS OF HEALTH

Health outcomes are determined by much more than a healthcare professional's interventions. Social determinants of health are conditions in the places where people live, learn, work, and play that affect a wide range of health and quality-of-life risks and outcomes.[9] Perhaps the most important social determinant of health is access: the ease of obtaining needed medical care. The US remains one of the only Western countries without a national or universal health system. The "US healthcare system" is a misnomer. The US health system is actually "US health systems."

Most Western countries have universal or national (one payer) healthcare systems, which include funding, policy, provision of care, and reimbursement. The US healthcare system is a disparate group of insurance plans including the military, Medicare, Medicaid, commercial, self-insured, and a variety of subplans including preferred provider organizations, accountable care organizations, health maintenance organizations, employer-sponsored plans, and high-deductible plans. All these plans, save for Medicare and the military plans, are individually regulated by the states. There is no federal oversight or ability to allocate services effectively. This leads to inefficiency, high administrative costs, and access issues. Reflect for a moment on the access issues faced by Americans simply by the myriad of health insurance plans and subplans as compared with a nation such as the United Kingdom with only one insurer, the National Health Service.

If we examine the pandemic as an objective exercise to measure the effectiveness, resilience, and efficacy of the US healthcare system, data infer that the US's response has been poor in many domains. One would expect—one would hope—that the intervention outcomes related to the common diagnosis of COVID-19 simultaneously affecting millions across this country would be equal in all geographic areas and among all races and ethnicities. However, we know that is not true. Early on in the pandemic, the pathogen hospitalized and killed African American/Black, Asian, and Hispanic persons at a much greater frequency than Caucasian persons, regardless of geographic area. Figure Two describes the fluctuating disparity of outcomes from COVID-19 based upon race.

Figure Two: COVID-19 Weekly Deaths per 100,000 Population by Race/Ethnicity, United States[10]

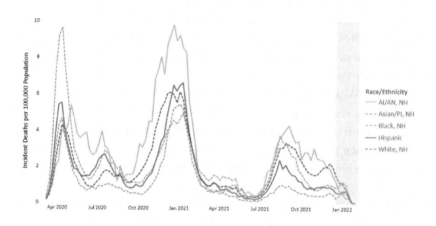

COVID-19, LEADERSHIP, AND THE POLITICIZATION OF HEALTH

COVID-19 has led to historic politicization of science and health-care. Science and health have typically been viewed with an objective vision. Scientists, using time-honored, regimented, evidence-based research design, methodology, statistical analysis, and control of con-founding variables, produced data and conclusions that were previously unquestioned by the public. The result of scientific inquiry was accepted due to the diligence and scientific expertise of researchers.

For some reason, in the time of COVID-19, science and research results have come under attack for political gains. How heartbreaking it has been to witness the noble Dr. Anthony Fauci, despite his exemplary record as a bench researcher, immunologist, physician, Director of the US National Institute of Allergy and Infectious Diseases, and chief med-ical advisor to the president, be excoriated by particular cohorts within American society for simply telling the truth, as scientists are supposed to do. Even as of the writing of this manuscript, Dr. Fauci continues to be under attack by elements of American politics.[11] Similar politiciza-tion has occurred with conclusions and recommendations from the Centers for Disease Control and Prevention, certain medical journals' editorial boards, and the National Institutes of Health.

COVID-19 AND HEALTHCARE SYSTEM RESILIENCY

COVID-19 produced a much-needed wake-up call to the US healthcare system in the domain of resiliency. In 2020, at the height of the pandemic, we witnessed grave concerns within the medical community that if the pandemic worsened, there would be no empty hospital beds to harbor persons with COVID-19. We learned that there were insufficient ventilators and positive pressure isolation rooms to support patients with COVID-19. We saw hospitals competing against hospitals and states competing against states for the purchase of personal protective equipment such as gowns and N-95 masks. Even as of this writing in mid-2021, more than a year after the beginning of the pandemic, many hospital personnel are still required to "bag and reuse" their PPE due to chronic shortages. Many of the shortages can be traced to the movement of US manufacturing overseas to save production costs and increase company profits. Once the pandemic arrived, supply chains were disrupted, and America no longer had the ability to quickly manufacture these devices.

COVID-19 AND LEADERSHIP

In Washington, DC and across the nation, the president, members of Congress, and state governors were seen on the evening news contradicting each other regarding mask and social distancing mandates, "closing" sections of the economy, and the need to close or reopen schools, often at the behest of certain political parties and ideologies. This constant mixed messaging confused the average American citizen, which led to zig-zagging behavior, which in turn led to a worsening of the pandemic and death toll.

In October 2020, the editors of the *New England Journal of Medicine*, a respected medical journal with a very high impact factor, published an extraordinary opinion piece excoriating US political leaders for a lack of leadership during the pandemic. The authors wrote:

> *The United States came into this crisis with enormous advantages. Along with tremendous manufacturing capacity, we have a biomedical research system that is the envy of the world. We have enormous expertise in public health,*

health policy, and basic biology and have consistently been able to turn that expertise into new therapies and preventive measures. And much of that national expertise resides in government institutions. Yet our leaders have largely chosen to ignore and even denigrate experts.

The response of our nation's leaders has been consistently inadequate. The federal government has largely abandoned disease control to the states. Governors have varied in their responses, not so much by party as by competence. But whatever their competence, governors do not have the tools that Washington controls. Instead of using those tools, the federal government has undermined them. The Centers for Disease Control and Prevention, which was the world's leading disease response organization, has been eviscerated and has suffered dramatic testing and policy failures. The National Institutes of Health have played a key role in vaccine development but have been excluded from much crucial government decision making. And the Food and Drug Administration has been shamefully politicized, appearing to respond to pressure from the administration rather than scientific evidence. Our current leaders have undercut trust in science and in government, causing damage that will certainly outlast them. Instead of relying on expertise, the administration has turned to uninformed "opinion leaders" and charlatans who obscure the truth and facilitate the promulgation of outright lies.[12]

As mentioned earlier, the US remains one of the few OECD countries without a national or universal health system. From a high of 48 million uninsured Americans in 2010, dropping to 28 million in 2016 (following enactment of the Affordable Care Act [ACA]), and rising to 30 million in early 2020 after parts of the ACA were gutted, a large number of Americans struggle to obtain healthcare.[13] Ironically, the federal government recognized these numbers and has determined that receiving the COVID-19 vaccines is a right of all citizens, but it has yet to recognize that routine and emergent healthcare are also an inherent right of citizens.

COVID-19 AND HEALTHCARE WORKERS

COVID-19 has been a sentinel event for healthcare workers. Though exact numbers may never be known, there are estimates that hundreds of US healthcare workers succumbed to infections from COVID-19 obtained while working with COVID-19-positive patients. Anecdotally, a relatively large number of healthcare workers have left the profession, victims of professional burnout or frustration, due to the unwillingness of Americans to comply with evidence-based precautions to avoid infection. Healthcare professionals have expressed anger at citizens who have developed COVID-19 infections due to unwillingness to comply with behavioral standards and thus place healthcare workers at risk.[14]

CONCLUSION

In summary, COVID-19 has been a sentinel event within our healthcare system. America has learned, often tragically, that a poorly functioning, unreliable, and non-resilient healthcare system, coupled with politicization and ineffective leadership, can lead to extensive and long-standing disruptions to many aspects of society. Hopefully, when the next pandemic occurs—and one most assuredly will—the US will have taken to heart many of the lessons learned from COVID-19.

CHAPTER 8

From Crimea to COVID-19, We Nurses Are What We Do

BY DEBORAH WHITTAKER

Florence Nightingale was an exceptional individual. She stepped away from a life of comfort and privilege in society to care for the sick, wounded, and helpless during the Crimean War in the 1850s. We affectionately refer to her as "the lady with the lamp." As a nurse, she tended wounded soldiers, night and day, and she was also an early "light" among researchers. Her observations, statistics, and critical thinking led to her *Notes on Nursing*, her book written in 1859 that remains a must-read for all nurses today. She is considered to be the founder of nursing.

Just as Florence Nightingale taught young women during her time to be nurses, we at DeSales University continue that tradition of educating women and men to become exceptional nurses. Our journey began with the first baccalaureate nursing class graduating in 1978, and today we offer undergraduate, graduate, and doctoral degrees in nursing. Our Division mission statement builds on Nightingale's foundations of nursing and challenges us to make a difference domestically and globally, which is completely appropriate for our current pandemic:

The mission of the Division of Nursing at DeSales University is to prepare professional, caring, competent undergraduate and graduate nursing students who have the ability to improve domestic and global health outcomes in the

Salesian tradition of Christian humanism. Graduates are prepared to assume clinical, leadership, and diverse healthcare positions to contribute to the advancement of nursing and other healthcare professions. Graduates are prepared to further their individual advancement through future academic endeavors and lifelong learning.

Nurses are always ready for the unexpected. It's how we were educated and prepared. As nursing educators, we've completed graduate studies, many at the doctoral level. We've published clinical and academic research, have extensive clinical practice with specialty certifications, and have years of experiences that we are thrilled to share with our students. Don't ask us what we think about a healthcare topic unless you're ready to spend a lot of time listening and discussing the current evidence as we base our practice on evidence-based research.

Many of us remember working with HIV positive patients before we knew how this horrible condition was transmitted and treated. We worked with patients, who had mental health conditions that were not yet diagnosed or treated, in a respectful manner, without judgment and with dignity. We have learned a lot over our years as nurses, and we've grown to be faithful advocates for those who need us. Our voices are united, strong, and we can be relentless as warriors, from the critical care wards to university classrooms. Just ask any of our colleagues.

We can look back on the arrival of the COVID-19 pandemic with a sense of pride and inspired accomplishment. In the fall semester of 2019, we were educating our nursing students as we normally do, when a virus known as "COVID-19" was mentioned in the news, but consistently downplayed as to what it could mean for us and our country. As its momentum grew and its seriousness was realized, we started to get our first glimpse that life as we knew it was going to change. In true nursing fashion, our faculty started working literally "24/7," with emails, phone calls, and Zoom sessions, to develop a plan of action. Immediately, the consensus was to help our students receive the best education, stay safe during the pandemic, and still provide care to as many patients as allowed.

Our attitude in 2020 was, "Of course we can do this. We'll figure this out, we're nurses!" The administrative staff supported our efforts, and we quickly moved from on-campus learning and in-hospital clinical, to a totally online educational experience that included simulated clinical experiences. Our students did not miss one day of learning.

We used avatar-style computer clinical simulations, as well as "live" standardized patients (real people from the community who role play a specific health condition or situation). We created our own "tele-health" experience with our campus simulation team, and students were able to care for standardized patients from their homes via their computers, on camera, while faculty observed, evaluated, and taught from those experiences. Our clinical nursing adjunct faculty stayed onboard with us, learning the new simulation technology, meeting with their clinical groups weekly to debrief and discuss their simulated experiences. We were so proud of our division, students, and adjuncts for their response, yet we had no idea our biggest moment was yet to come.

As nurses, we had to get back into the hospital. Our students were adamant that they wanted to return to the clinical setting and take care of patients. They were not going to run from the pandemic; they were going to meet it head-on. They wanted to help their fellow nurses, many of whom were DeSales nursing graduates. Our students had read and seen on television how hard nurses were working—the long hours, the lack of breaks, no days off—and their hearts were full. We faculty were so proud of their response, and so we worked with our hospital systems and suppliers to get them equipped and ready.

To begin with, students all needed N-95 masks and to be fit-tested. There was no "one size fits all," and it was extremely important to have a tight, correct fit to keep the wearer safe from contracting an airborne disease such as COVID-19. Then they added a surgical mask on top of the N-95. When hospitals received enough personal protective equipment (PPE), they had access to gowns, gloves, and goggles to wear as necessary. Once nursing faculty and students received the COVID-19 vaccinations, we were ready to jump into the fight of the worst pandemic of our lifetimes and make a difference in as many lives as possible.

From February 2021, we returned to all clinicals, apart from the designated COVID-19 units and aerosolized procedures per current hospital requirements. DeSales nurses served in medical/surgical, pediatric, obstetric, and mental health units. So many of these units were short-staffed because of emergency demands, disease, and burn-out. The threat of COVID-19 was not confined to the COVID-19 units. At any time, in any area, a patient or hospital staff member could start to manifest symptoms or spread the disease unknowingly when unmasked. The infection could have been picked up from anywhere, including outside the hospital, where vaccines or testing was lacking, or protocols such as social distancing, masking, and handwashing were not consistently followed.

Of course, there were emotional, unnerving moments. Of course, there were scary, uncertain situations. However, we were determined to practice what we preach. We had scientific evidence; we knew how this virus was transmitted, how to protect ourselves, and how to treat patients safely and compassionately. We could provide safe, quality patient care and demonstrate compassion and humanity, the way we teach our students. As we returned to clinical settings, a new opportunity presented itself for our students and faculty.

The hospitals needed us to help vaccinate. Community members, most of them elderly, were waiting over an hour in line to receive their vaccines. Many students and several faculty were able to take on this request, on top of their studies—and for the faculty, in addition to working fulltime already. Working side by side with our students to fight this pandemic is an experience that we will never forget. The knowing glances of compassion, hope, and sadness, as we heard the stories of the people in our vaccination chairs, were shared silently across our vaccination stations. The stories were of loss, isolation, and sadness, but also of hope and appreciation of kindness. We were thanked continuously for our service, bravery, and kindness. We thanked them for coming to see us, getting their vaccine, and for their bravery. As nurses do, we smiled and cried with each person. We just wished we could hug them.

So, as the pandemic grinds on, fighting to exist, with one variant after another, how should we move forward? We have to start with reflection, something generally undervalued by students but practiced by faculty. We look back at where we were, what we did, what went well and not so well, how we felt, how others felt, and how we made a difference. I would like to believe we made a positive contribution; we fought the pandemic, treated each other with understanding and compassion, and educated our students in a way previously unimagined. I can confidently say that our students met all their course and clinical outcomes. Seniors graduated and took their licensure examinations with good results. I know we did our best.

Based on reflection, we will continue to do our work as educators by being ready and open to change. Flexibility took on a new meaning during the pandemic. We could no longer consider the old way of doing things and instead embraced how to do things a new way. We must continue to be kind and compassionate individuals, to mentor and guide our students by our actions and words, as we all know that character counts. We must continue to find the joy in living our lives, in any way possible, even if it's not what we expected it to be. We can infuse joy, kindness, and compassion to all around us if we remember its importance, relying on our Christian faith to guide and support us, knowing that we are never truly alone. Small steps, simple words, or a gesture can mean more than we sometimes realize, making a difference in a person's life.

We all experienced the pandemic differently, and some people will have the scars long after the pandemic subsides. We need to take care of ourselves, physically, mentally, emotionally, and spiritually, if we are going to be able to care for others. We can be open with our hearts, laugh, cry, console, rejoice, nurture, support, care, and love. From Florence Nightingale in the Crimean war to today's COVID-19 pandemic war, we are nurses. It's what we do.

CHAPTER 9

Enhance the Human Connection in Medicine

BY BOBBIE MORICI

Human connection has been fundamental to medicine and patient care throughout history. *"Wherever the art of medicine is loved, there is also a love of humanity"* was penned by Hippocrates. *This underlying truth has carried on through medicine and remains a key element in effective patient care.* Human connection, contact, and touch, so sharply reduced in medical practice during the COVID-19 pandemic, needs to be restored in full and strengthened to allow for better patient care.

The importance of human interaction in medicine is integral in the process of training students to be compassionate providers. Of the Accreditation Council for Graduate Medical Education (ACGME) six endorsed core competencies for medical trainees, three involve the importance of the connection between the provider and the patient: patient care, interpersonal and communication skills, and professionalism.[1] Patient care requires that providers participate in care that is compassionate, appropriate, and effective. Interpersonal and communication skills seek effective communication with patients, their families, and other members of the healthcare team. Professionalism requires a respect for ethical principles and a sensitivity to patient diversity. These three competencies mirror the competencies of the physician assistant profession.[2]

Any diminution of this basic need in medicine has far-reaching impacts on both patients and providers. These effects are demonstrated through the impact on patients in the provider-patient relationship, the impact on providers through their job satisfaction and emotional well-being, and the significance of family and friends in the healing of patients. We cannot always qualitatively measure the impact of human touch and connection on healing for patients and emotional well-being for medical providers, but we can create a care environment where the human connection remains the center of patient care.

Prior to the COVID-19 pandemic, the broad utilization of technology in medicine created environments where human connection can be overlooked. The innovation of electronic health records (EHR) can lead providers to focus more on the computer screen than on the patient if training is not properly conducted. The utilization of telemedicine can lead to cold and impersonal interactions if not made to center on the person-to-person connection. The increasing use of the technological advancements that have made treating, curing, and healing many patients possible can lead to a lack of empathetic interactions if not properly infused into the treatment plan.

Studies have explored the impact that these advancements in medicine have had on the provider-patient relationship. A 2018 observational study of primary care and specialty consultations demonstrated that patients may be less-active participants in medical encounters when providers are engrossed in their computer screens. The authors suggest that providers maintain conversation while utilizing the EHR to keep the patient engaged and improve the patient-provider interpersonal experience.[3] Utilizing techniques to keep patients engaged in visits, whether in-person with EHR or via telemedicine, may be the key to maintaining the human connection. A study of 38,609 Press Ganey patient satisfaction surveys following telemedicine visits during COVID-19 revealed that satisfaction can be maintained with telemedicine. The researchers uncovered significantly higher satisfaction scores for the telemedicine patients when compared to in-office visits over the same time period, one year prior to COVID-19.[4] These studies provide hope that with proper training and utilization, we can uncover ways to incorporate EHR and medical technology into patient interactions while maintaining meaningful personal connections.

While the importance of connecting with patients has been known for centuries, the ability to see the effects of medicine without this human connection has presented itself only recently. During the COVID-19 pandemic, many providers were forced to learn ways to practice medicine while safeguarding themselves from contracting this deadly virus. Adjustments were made to patient care delivery as a necessity to preserve our medical force. Outpatient visits were transitioned to telemedicine whenever possible to avoid unnecessary face-to-face contact. Hospital equipment was housed in hallways to limit the amount of time that nurses and providers needed to spend in the patient's room. Many visits were conducted via phone with limited physical exposure to the patient to adhere to the Centers for Disease Control and Prevention's guidelines regarding exposure to COVID-19 patients. These steps were necessary and allowed many medical providers to maintain their own health in order to provide care.

Many providers creatively adjusted their daily routines to find ways to provide this powerful healing to patients. Because nurses were not allowed to touch patients' hands, they crafted hands to hold from two rubber gloves blown up and placed on the dorsal and palmar aspects of a patient's hand to soothe and comfort them. This is just one example of the creativity that providers utilized to mimic the connection that patients so desperately needed. Providers placed themselves at risk countless times to provide the care that patients needed, even if it exceeded recommended exposure times. Medical professionals did not abandon their desire to save their patients based on concerns for their own safety.

In *Let Us Dream*, Pope Francis recognizes that the choices of our medical professionals to place themselves in harm's way allows them to answer the call to serve others. He calls these caregivers "the saints next door" and "the antibodies to the virus of indifference." He reminds the reader that we grow by "losing ourselves in service."[5] The power of this message was most profoundly demonstrated by our healthcare workers who navigated the unknowns of this pandemic. Pope Francis stresses that we must let people's reality speak to us in order to truly serve them. He stresses the importance of letting the suffering around us speak to us and allowing God to reach us through this. Our healthcare community did just this. They found ways to rise above the changes in medicine that interfered with their ability to connect with their patients. They innovated, created, and loved beyond measure to continue to provide medical care, but, more importantly, human touch.

Finally, community lockdowns and quarantine rules prohibited patients from seeing and interacting with their families and friends. These restrictions on human interaction, while necessary, contributed additional hurdles for both patients and medical providers. Hospitals shut their doors to visitors, people shuttered themselves inside their homes, and the ability to care for an ill loved one was stripped away. An analysis of post-operative experiences of non-COVID-19 surgical patients demonstrated that patients who had no visitors were less satisfied with their hospital experience. A qualitative analysis of respondents in this study revealed that 50.8% of patients in the no-visitor cohort felt socially isolated as a result of the lack of psychosocial support.[6] While the visitation lockdown was largely necessary to protect patients, healthcare workers, and the community, the impacts of these policies can certainly impact patient satisfaction and outcomes. A meta-analysis of studies exploring patient outcomes during visitation restrictions revealed physical and mental consequences. Physically, patients reported more pain, worse personal hygiene, and worsening nutritional status during the visitation limits. Mentally, nursing home residents demonstrated more depressive symptoms, loneliness, and agitation during limited visitation. Similarly, family members across multiple studies reported increased worry, anxiety, and stress, as well as a feeling of "failing to support and protect their loved ones."[7]

As our society continues to navigate through the COVID-19 pandemic and strives toward life without restrictions, we must learn from the lessons of this pandemic and adapt our medical practice. As Pope Francis states, we must dare to dream of the path to a better future. This better future begins by remembering our commitments to provide quality, compassionate patient care. It begins by remembering the oaths that we have taken as healthcare providers, whether it is to do no harm or injustice, as cited in the Hippocratic Oath, or the various versions of this mantra that are stated in medical professional oaths. It begins by taking these vows that we pledged to adhere to and infusing them into our daily practice in meaningful ways. This new beginning will require more research to fully assess the impacts of the COVID-19 pandemic on our ability to connect personally as healthcare providers and patients. It will require support for each other, whether we are medical professionals, patients, or family members.

May the realization that human connection is integral to healing lead to more meaningful patient interactions that include eye contact, actively listening and engaging, and compassion for the humanness of our patients. May we, as providers, slow down our patient interactions and allow for more time to connect on a personal level. May we, as family members and caretakers, strive to be present and engaged in the medical care that our loved ones receive. May we, as patients, open our hearts to the suffering that medical providers have faced and approach our interactions with a mutual compassion for their dedication, sacrifice, and loving care. As Pope Francis notes, it will require us to open ourselves, decenter, and transcend. "And then act. Call up, go visit, offer your service. Say you don't have a clue what they do, but maybe you can help. Say you'd like to be part of a different world, and you thought this might be a good place to start."[8]

Infusing Joy in the Year of the Nurse

BY KAREN PETERSON

In January of 2019, the World Health Organization declared 2020 the year of the nurse and the midwife.[1] The designation stated that nurses play a vital role in providing health services. In November 2019, Dr. Richard Ricciardi, the new President of Sigma Theta Tau International Honor Society for Nurses, delivered his call to action at the Biennium in Washington, DC to nurse leaders throughout the world. He called on the members to infuse their work with joy, highlighting three essentials that promote it: "awareness, balance and purpose, and co-creation." He stated, "All healthcare workers face challenges that can trigger burnout, such as staffing shortages, incivility and violence, lack of control in the workplace, barriers to education, and misaligned policies and regulations."[2] Instead of accepting these problems as the status quo, he called on nurses to seize the opportunity to improve our experiences and work cultures.

Just a few short months later, the world was locked down due to a global pandemic. In March 2020, DeSales University, following Pennsylvania mandates, sent students home, and they did not return until that summer. How does one infuse joy in a pandemic?

This is not what was intended for the Year of the Nurse, but nurses throughout the world rose to the occasion as they always have. Although not on the front lines, those in academia felt it was essential to support the nurses who were. The question became, how can we help them, and what can we do? We chose to co-create opportunities in spite of the problems, just as Dr. Ricciardi called us to do.

Providing clinical placements for students in actual practice settings, a vital part of nursing education, became an area for co-creation. As the numbers of patients with COVID-19 increased in hospitals, it became clear that students would soon not be allowed, or have limited access, in clinical settings. Nursing faculty quickly changed track and provided online and simulation opportunities and alternatives to meet the objectives for our undergraduate and graduate courses. How could we do this for the final course for the graduate Clinical Nurse Specialist (CNS) tract that is held in the spring semester? These students are required to complete 225 clinical hours with a preceptor in this course. What options could we arrange that would provide meaningful experiences and not just a substitute? It is important to keep in mind as well that, in addition to their course work, these nurses were also practicing in hospitals where COVID-19 was real. Special attention needed to be made to care for them as nurses in addition to the course work.

The Clinical Nurse Specialist (CNS) is a master's prepared nurse who impacts three spheres of nursing.[3] The CNS may provide direct patient care, but they are also involved in education and program changes for nurses. The third area, which became even more important during COVID-19, was the sphere of the organization. A CNS can plan and implement organizational changes. Their expertise in this area was instrumental in making changes in care across a hospital setting that otherwise might have taken months.

The treatment and care of patients with COVID-19 changed quickly as the healthcare systems began to understand how the disease worked. As these changes, such as the need to "prone" (putting a patient on their stomach), were determined to save lives, nurses needed to be trained in order to prevent further injuries to the patient and to themselves. Policies and practice changes also needed to occur to expedite this throughout the organization. CNS education is focused on a nurse being able to impact these three areas quickly. The final course in our program is focused on providing opportunities for a student to gain expertise in practice in the organizational sphere.

As the faculty member teaching the course, it was important for me to determine how we could meet this outcome without a clinical practice setting. Demonstration of the CNS competency of collaboration would also be difficult to evaluate without a team to work with. In order to meet the course outcomes and allow the students to demonstrate competency in organizational problem solving and collaboration, simulation was determined to be a possible solution.

Simulation experiences are viewed as opportunities to provide experience and are an accepted practice in nursing and other healthcare related fields.[4] In a review of the literature related to the CNS, it was discovered that there were few prepared simulations for CNSs and none that focused on the organizational sphere of impact. They needed to be developed. So, with the help of the DeSales Nursing Simulation Specialist, five cases were developed to meet the students' needs.

In one type of simulation experience, manikins are used and in other simulations actual people, called Standardized Patients, are used to portray patient symptoms and problems. For the new CNS scenarios, the roles of the Standardized Patients were redesigned to portray people other than patients, to help the students practice in an organization. These people played roles such as chief operating officers, risk managers, community health workers, and social workers. These Standardized People (SP) were not nurses and had not played these roles before. Training was provided for the cases and the roles in coordination with the DeSales Simulation Center. Due to COVID-19, this was all done virtually.

In a virtual format, each student was presented with one of the five new cases, each of which was a systems problem to manage. They collaborated with their fellow students to develop a plan that would solve the problem in all three spheres. They presented the plan to the SP and worked within the simulated organization.

The students reported the experience as extremely helpful in allowing them to function in the organization. The students were able to meet their course and clinical outcomes in a positive manner. These were so positive that the cases were again used when the course repeated in the spring of 2021, and six additional cases were developed to use in the initial course for the CNS, which focuses on Health Care

Disparities and Social Determinants of Health. This focus became even more important when increased mortality and difference in treatment results in COVID-19 were a direct result of these disparities.

The creation of new and innovative strategies in education for nursing students is one example of how to answer the call and to seize an opportunity in a time of crisis to improve what is currently being done. These simulations will continue to be used long after we return to a post-pandemic world.

Mu Omicron, the DeSales Chapter for Sigma Nursing Honor Society, took the call to heart as well. Mental Health Issues are also increasing in this time of crisis. The members of the chapter had already begun a collaboration with local chapters as well as with the students from Cedar Crest College, Moravian University, and Chestnut Hill College. Three years ago (2019), these three institutions met on the DeSales Campus to host an Out of Darkness Campus Walk to bring awareness to suicide assessment and prevention.

The American Foundation for Suicide Prevention assists in providing tools to help the teams get started in raising funds, providing education, and supporting those who have experienced suicide as family members, friends, or professionals.[5] The Walk happened virtually in April of 2020 and was considered a success. With a slow reopening and continued COVID-19 infections, the teams pondered how to make the Walk happen in 2021. In September 2020, the teams began to plan and did not allow the pandemic to interfere with the goal to provide support to those suffering and raise money for prevention and education.

In spite of the pandemic, the Out of Darkness Walk increased participation from the three schools to include three more schools, became the Lehigh Valley Campus Walk, and added the support of the Lehigh Valley Health Network. Participants from as far away as California and Florida participated with monetary support as well as attending the walk virtually. The program was ultimately held live on campus and streamed with the help of our Conference Services to others across the country. The walk raised $48,600 to continue this essential support, placing fourth in the country in total amount raised. Due to the increased size of the event, we plan to host a live walk in April 2022 in the Lehigh Valley Parkway.

It was not just the walk that made a difference. In preparation, the chapter sponsored a program for discussing suicide among college students and how to recognize and provide assistance for those who need help. The documentary film *Out of Sight: Stop the Stigma, Start a Conversation*, directed by Kyle Mahaney, a DSU TV-Film student, was shown on campus to help us remember to talk about the problem, to pull it out of the dark and into the light. In addition to this program, the chapter sponsored a streamed conference discussing "Substance Use in the Valley." The proceedings were recorded and serve as an educational resource that helps support healthcare providers and students in their care of those with mental health and substance abuse issues. Not to be deterred by a pandemic, the Mu Omicron Chapter took on another project with the Gift of Life Challenge for organ and tissue donation. In coordination with the Division of Business, DeSales University placed third in the number of donors obtained. We met this challenge as well.

Although joy may not be something that comes to mind when we think of the COVID-19 pandemic, we can heed the call to look for opportunities to improve what we have and to do more to help those that have felt the effects of the pandemic. Healthcare providers have been on the front lines now for over a year. The number of cases has decreased, only to surge again with each new variant.

Healthcare providers have worked long and hard. Many have given up nursing, and many have experienced moral injury in decisions that needed to be made about patients and their care. Many experience symptoms of post-traumatic stress disorder.[6] One way to support those experiencing trauma is through circle process. Circle process is not a therapy, nor does it have a designated leader. It is an opportunity to share and to heal.[7] It has been used in a variety of settings, including with veterans, to help with recovery from moral injury and trauma. Circle processes work as a healing practice and are being offered through Mu Omicron Chapter to those who are interested in talking about their experience.

Although we in academia were not all on the front line, many of us felt guilty about not being there to help and support our friends and colleagues. We have tried to do what we could to support those who were. When the vaccine came out, it was with great pride and honor that we went to the vaccine clinics and assisted in administering thousands of vaccines—an opportunity not soon forgotten, as people said, "Thank you for being here for us."

The Year of the Nurse may not have looked like what it was supposed to be, but it has been a year for honoring those on the front lines. Their role in the pandemic will not soon be forgotten. They have been honored in a variety of ways with parades, posters, and banners, and in large ceremonies such as the New York City Parade and the World Series.

This is how we answered the call and infused joy. As nurses, we rose to the challenge in whatever capacity we could. We collaborated with others and developed new plans and ways of doing things. We focused on becoming more knowledgeable and fighting for those with healthcare disparities and social determinants that affect health, especially those with mental illness.

We have a long road ahead of us. COVID-19 variants continue to change, and our response must change with it. We must recognize the long road ahead, with PTSD, burnout, and staff shortages in our healthcare settings. The battle is not over, and we must continue to seize the opportunity to make changes and improve healthcare. We will continue to look for ways to make a difference. After all, 2021 was designated, again, as the Year of the Nurse.

CHAPTER 11

COVID-19: A Mental Health 9/11 for College Students

BY JACQUELINE OCHSENREITHER

The college years have long been recognized to coincide with mental health problems such as substance abuse, mood disorders, and psychosis, which may lead to increased suicidal thoughts and acts in college-age high-risk populations.[1] A study of 155,026 college-age students from 196 US campuses from 2007 to 2017 revealed a significant increase in rates of mental health treatment, new diagnoses of a lifetime mental health condition, depression, and thoughts of suicide.[2]

For many college students with substantial mental health concerns, coupled with escalating feelings of depression, anxiety, and lack of access to care, the onset of the global pandemic in March 2020 led to overwhelming hardships and stressors that further isolated them from friends, teachers, colleagues, and mental health treatments. This is especially true for the non-traditional (NT) student.

Non-traditional students coordinate between essential employment obligations, family responsibilities, and schoolwork, all while managing their own mental health needs, concerns, and challenges related to the COVID-19 pandemic.

Are college students in a mental health state of emergency, similar to what people experienced in our country post-9/11? Will universities be able to support students with resiliency and coping strategies that help mitigate feelings of anxiety, depression, loneliness, and frustration? Will college students successfully navigate the pandemic-infused college landscapes, always "pivoting," faces at half-mask? Will we spear-head the important task of understanding the long-term effects of COVID-19 on mental health as it relates to college students, beyond the initial months and the first decade, similar to 9/11?

College faculty, administrators, families, and mental health provid-ers, now more than ever, are essential in recognizing, supporting, and providing care to all college students suffering from the ongoing men-tal health effects and losses experienced from the COVID-19 pandemic.

MAJOR CHALLENGES OF COLLEGE STUDENTS DURING COVID-19

A global pandemic declaration was made by the World Health Organization on March 11, 2020, for coronavirus COVID-19.[3] Academic institutions of higher learning closed campuses, directed residen-tial students home, and transitioned educational offerings to online learning in light of the threat and high risk of transmission.[4] As the pandemic raged over the following seventeen months, college students were faced with multiple challenges such as social distancing, mask wearing, and returning home yet again due to outbreaks of COVID-19 on college campuses. Some students who returned home were met with volatile circumstances, due to escalating family violence or unsupportive relatives and communities, most specifically in the case of LGBTQ+ youths.[5] Notably, housing and food insecurities provided additional stressors for students who relied solely on campus accom-modations due to ongoing college closures or travel restrictions.[6]

College students are rarely recognized as a priority population for health initiatives due to the misperception that they are healthy, privileged, and well-resourced. However, they are an underserved population with unique healthcare needs inclusive of escalating mental health disparities, namely anxiety and depression.[7] In 2019, the American College Health Association (ACHA) reported that 25% of the college student population has been treated or diagnosed with depression or anxiety within the previous twelve months. Addition-ally, suicide has been identified as the second-leading cause of death among college students.[8] The COVID-19 pandemic and its ongoing effects on college students' academic success, financial stability, housing and food security, and personal distress may lead to escalating risk factors compounding anxiety, depression, and thoughts of suicide in an already vulnerable population.[9]

COLLEGE STUDENT GRIEF AND LOSS RELATED TO COVID-19

Research has identified that feelings or symptoms of grief can be associated with death of a loved-one or with non-death losses.[10] Non-death losses for many college students related to the COVID-19 pandemic have included loss of employment, connection, academic experience, and ritual.[11] Many college students have experienced additional non-death losses related to cancelled ceremonial events such as graduations and inductions. The inability to focus on schoolwork and difficulty in adjusting to online learning from on-campus education were also reported as additional non-death losses for college students during the COVID-19 pandemic.[12]

Sirrine, Kliner, and Gollery, in a cross-sectional study, identified the most common non-death losses from the COVID-19 pandemic experienced by undergraduate and graduate college students in twelve US states: loss of normalcy (90.1%), change in educational delivery (85.8%), loss of connection to others/isolation (82.7%), and loss of ritual including graduations, weddings, etc. (60.5%).[13] Over 10% of participants experienced death of a loved one to COVID-19, and over 25% reported the death of a loved one caused by something other than COVID-19. Over 84% of participants stated that the COVID-19 pandemic had significantly impacted their lives and a statistically significant negative correlation was identified between educational classification and impact of COVID-19 on educational experience. Specifically, graduate students experienced less disruption in educational delivery or experience than undergraduate students. This could be related to age, maturity, or familiarity with online teaching modalities. However, students who reported more losses overall experienced increased loss of control and avoidance behaviors than their peers.[14]

Multiple losses or significant grief negatively impact individuals, especially college students. It has been previously reported that individuals who have experienced multiple losses may take longer to process grief and require ongoing supports and coping strategies to help manage feelings of pain and suffering.[15] Sirrine's study also found that college students who utilized spirituality and religious coping reported lower levels of avoidance and loss of control. These findings may support that spirituality can be a positive coping mechanism for loss and grief among college students during the COVID-19 pandemic.

EFFECT OF COVID-19 ON COLLEGE STUDENTS WITH DISABILITIES

College students with disabilities represent 19.4% of all traditional undergraduate students in the US.[16] It has been reported that this select group of college students may be experiencing more isolation than previously encountered, with ongoing restrictions and challenges related to the COVID-19 pandemic. Despite escalating isolation concerns, disabled students may have increased misgivings about returning to college campuses due to a greater likelihood of adverse health outcomes related to COVID-19 and co-morbid health conditions.

Students with disabilities have experienced even more challenges with the rapid transition to online learning during the COVID-19 pandemic, inclusive of new communication methods with instructors and peers, access to library resources, and technology support.[17] Of note, not all virtual educational options are truly accessible and appropriate for some students with disabilities. Prolonged screen time for classes or virtual meetings has been found to trigger migraines in some college students with disabilities, limiting participation and exposure to educational content and learning.[18]

Access to health services for college students with disabilities has been identified as an additional challenge for this specialized population during the COVID-19 pandemic. Students with disabilities who resided on-campus and relied on campus-based health services were limited in care or transitioned to virtual care, further restricting frequent engagement with healthcare providers, routinely required for this high-risk population. Disruption of services for this discrete population also included those requiring adaptive supports, such as wheelchairs. Virtual visits may not have facilitated adequate assessment of disabled students requiring these resources or others, since select disabled students experience vision, hearing, fine, and gross motor challenges as well.[19] Additionally, psychiatric disorders have been identified as one of the top three co-morbid diagnoses among students with disabilities.[20] Increased mental health support and access to care are paramount for this distinctive college student population.

Achieving educational equity for students with disabilities must remain a high priority, especially during times of crisis. Ensuring accessibility to educational learning via standard or adaptive equipment, remote or on-campus teaching and tutoring modalities, and providing mental and physical healthcare services, specifically targeting feelings of escalating isolation, anxiety, and depression in this select group of students, may best support this minority group during the ongoing COVID-19 pandemic, protecting their rights and access to equitable educational experiences and healthcare.

NON-TRADITIONAL COLLEGE STUDENTS' MENTAL HEALTH AND WELL-BEING AND COVID-19

Non-traditional college students make up a unique a group of individuals seeking a college degree. Non-traditional students have been defined by the US Department of Education as greater than 25 years of age, possibly a single parent, with a dependent other than a partner, enrolled in college part-time, possesses a high school diploma or GED, delayed college entry, financially independent, and/or working fulltime while attending college.[21] This vulnerable student population, due to additional life stressors inclusive of work, family, and financial demands, may be especially impacted by the COVID-19 pandemic. Additional challenges some NT students face include learning to use modern technologies, experiencing cultural or linguistic barriers, lacking confidence, and maintaining a healthy work/life balance.[22]

The ongoing COVID-19 pandemic and associated influences on job, food, and housing security may negatively impact the NT college student's ability to continue college enrollment or graduate, or it may delay future attendance. Not surprisingly, it has been reported in research literature that NT students have higher levels of anxiety, depression, and stress than their peers.[23] Another study reports that pre-pandemic, NT students were twice as likely to withdraw from college during or after their first year (38%) than their traditional counterparts (16%).[24] Their most significant source of stress has been reported to be between school and work/family.[25] Babb's quantitative, descriptive, correlational research examined the impact of COVID-19 on the well-being and mental health of traditional and NT college students in a single, urban, nonresidential university in the southeastern US. That study identifies a statistically significant difference in depression levels, anxiety, well-being, insomnia, and sleep quality from pre-pandemic to present among groups. COVID-19 has negatively impacted both traditional and NT students' overall mental health. Additionally, NT students were identified as more likely to experience sleep disturbances and insomnia than traditional students, due to higher levels of stress related to family and work responsibilities.[26]

COLLEGE STUDENT SUPPORT SERVICES RELATED TO COVID-19

Campus-based resources to address high-priority concerns of all college students affected by COVID-19 and the ongoing pandemic are imperative in order to support healing and coping during this very volatile time. Provision of campus resources such as telehealth, text-messaging, or weekly peer-networking and/or mental health sessions that directly address social distancing and associated feelings of isolation in college students may deescalate feelings of anxiety and depression in this vulnerable population.

Off-campus housing with food resources for quarantined-specific, isolation-required, travel-restricted, or volatile/family-circumstanced students, provided by college officials for students in need, may offset students' stressors of food and housing insecurity if pandemic parameters worsen. For students with disabilities, maintenance of educational, psychosocial, and healthcare equity requires optimization, so that learning and academic success can be supported for this unique group of students during the ongoing pandemic and beyond.

Healthcare is pivotal for all students, especially during times of crisis. On-campus and telehealth healthcare and mental health services are essential to address the impact on well-being, feelings of loss, and grief reactions students and faculty may feel with the ongoing pandemic.

The assessment of death and non-death loss among college students and faculty and how past and present circumstances and stressors are impacting overall feelings of loss and grief reactions is crucial.

Mental health supports that specifically address those who have experienced significant death loss and non-death losses related to COVID-19 should be integrated into college campus offerings. Provision of coping modalities that address resilience and healing are vital and should be discussed with all faculty and students. Courses integrated into core curricula that build on resilience strategy and positive reappraisal to support those with losses during the pandemic, especially cumulative, may be helpful for faculty and students alike.

Psychosocial spiritual supports have been found to improve coping and resilience in college students.[27] Fostering and promoting spiritual practices specifically targeting coping among faculty and students may best be utilized and organized at faith-based universities or colleges. Faith-based organizations may consider the utilization of grief and spiritualty assessments, in concert with other secular and resilience coping strategies, to support faculty and students dealing with feelings of isolation, anxiety, depression, and loss associated with COVID-19.

Prioritizing the mental health needs of college students, now more than ever, is a critical role for college faculty, administrators, families, and mental health providers. Empathically engaging with students is vital in order to be able to respond and support their feelings of loss, anxiety, and stress related to the ongoing COVID-19 pandemic.

CHAPTER 12

Pandemic Education: Burning Fire to Superbloom?

BY KATRIN BLAMEY

There is no doubt that the 2020–2021 pandemic has irrevocably changed the field of Education. While some effects were immediately identifiable, others remain dormant and will emerge as generations of affected students make their way through the school system. In this way, the experience can be likened to a forest fire.

The spark was March 2020, when schools across the globe shuttered their classrooms seemingly overnight in response to the immediate health crisis. Unlike anything they had trained for or even imagined in their wildest dreams, teachers had to grow into a different kind of educator—one who worked from home and entered students' private spaces through a web-camera lens. The reality is that only a small percentage of cyber school educators had experience with full remote delivery of instruction prior to this complete shift.

The fire analogy continues as the pandemic school year became a slow, yet uncontrollable burn. School administrators, teachers, parents, and politicians dug in with opposing beliefs over the mechanics of safely delivering a quality education to students of all ages. Schoolboard meetings across the country turned into yelling matches and bitter battles to either remain virtual or reinstate in-person learning. At the same time, teachers, students, and parents struggled to adapt to the new learning spaces of Zoom, Microsoft Teams, and Google Classroom.

Preliminary data suggests that students suffered the most in terms of educational learning outcomes. Academic assessment data reports skyrocketing failure rates among middle and high school students, sometimes in the range of double and triple increases from failures prior to the pandemic. Elementary school teachers report anecdotally seeing young readers up to 9 months behind in literacy skills from where they should be at any given time of year in kindergarten. And the burn continues, as schools slowly wind down the academic year with hopes of returning to a more normal experience in coming semesters.

The transformative change that the field of Education is currently undergoing concludes our forest fire analogy with the stage of regeneration. After all, a forest fire, while destructive and awful at its largest, brings change and new growth to the forest floor in its wake. Nutrients from the dead trees are returned to the soil. More sunlight reaches new seedlings as the canopy thins. And occasionally, in rare instances, the reborn forest experiences a superbloom when the ground is suddenly covered by vibrant purple and pink wildflowers that sprout out of the ash. It remains to be seen if our pandemic education will result in a superbloom, but there is reason to hope.

Predicting the superbloom in the floor of ash is a speculative undertaking. However, there is at least one area in which the pandemic has fundamentally reinforced a truth educators always knew but had forgotten in the assessment-driven, technology-infused landscape of modern schooling. The truth is quite simple: Education is an act of human connection. Pandemic education has reinforced quite clearly that the connection between a teacher and a student is an essential, critical component of the learning process.

Consider the state of education at the heart of the full shutdown, when students and parents were home, with education mostly occurring through self-paced asynchronous assignments delivered, in the best-case scenarios, in weekly teacher-created tasks, and in the worst-case scenarios, in the form of packets photocopied and offered for pick-up in front of school buildings. Taking the teacher out of the equation completely, students' education rapidly fell apart. Without the teacher to motivate, encourage, and support, many students just stopped learning altogether. This phenomenon can be compared to the heavily researched summer slump, in which the three months of summer off from school result in a regression in learning outcomes. One of the most devastating effects of the pandemic will be the educational loss in an entire generation of students. Parents' experiences reinforced this conclusion as many quickly realized they could not teach their own children.

As the pandemic set in and communities determined that we were in this for the long haul, one of the loudest cries was for schools to reopen in some capacity for their students. A cynical view might be that parents simply needed their children out of the way so they could focus on the duties of working from home. However, the more charitable view is that parents, like teachers, quickly concluded that their children needed someone with knowledge of how to teach: not just how to get tasks done, but how to guide learning. By living through at-home learning, parents gained a newfound understanding of just how hard teaching can be.

Schools around the country first came back to synchronous education via technology, in the form of Zoom or Microsoft Team meetings. At last, the human teacher was back in front of the classroom, although a virtual classroom. While certainly a step in the right direction, this too proved to be a problematic learning environment. First, not every student was included. Inequity in educational opportunities based on socioeconomic status, race, home language, and learning ability was a known problem pre-pandemic. However, the pandemic shone a brighter spotlight on differences in the kinds of educational opportunities that some students have over others. It was hard to ignore the clear fact that some students could learn because they had access to computers with stable internet connections and others could not. Clearer still was the news that some students could learn because they were fed at home and others could not. Many school officials became ground zero, not for educational distribution, but first and foremost, for food distribution.

The differences in educational opportunities aside, the Zoom learning environment did not meet the needs of all those learners who had access to it. The human teacher was there, but the human connection was not. Why? Many new Zoomers experienced the fatigue of online meetings, the physical drain of being camera-ready, and the sheer exhaustion of talking to an image of a human without the reinforcement of human touch, nonverbal communication cues, and eye contact. Multiply this by 25 students, and you have a virtual classroom environment. Teachers scrambled to translate the best of their lesson plans into something that would work in an online space. Hands-on activities became virtual manipulatives. Read Alouds became recordings with slide presentations. And small group, peer collaboration occurred in breakout rooms where students were disengaged, too embarrassed to talk to one another, fatigued, or unsure of what to do on their own. In many early childhood classrooms, precious instructional time dissolved into constant reminders from the teacher to "turn your cameras on."

Without the actual, physical connection with the teacher, all the same learning methods just did not work the same way. Across countless schools, the most effective teachers quickly realized two important things. First, in order to make the online learning space work for them, they would have to go back to basics to reestablish connections with students. Second, they needed to get students back into the classroom as soon as safely possible. A "we are all in this together" mentality began to reshape virtual classrooms. Teachers began to find humor and things to celebrate; new conversations were begun with students to find out about how they were doing mentally, emotionally, and as a whole being; and families were newly engaged in the learning of their children.

As many schools have begun the process of transitioning yet again from virtual to hybrid to mostly in-person, lessons learned from the pandemic can be the system's superbloom. Clearly, the pandemic has had a cumulative negative impact on the education of individual students, but educators can learn from their experiences during pandemic education. There are valuable takeaways to remember moving forward:

1. *Teaching is challenging, and not everyone can do it successfully.*

2. *Educational opportunities are not always equitable.*

3. *Teachers need parents who are allies in their children's education.*

4. *Learning is a process of human connection.*

Rather than return completely to a pre-pandemic state, schools have the potential to emerge stronger. A post-pandemic school could be the place where community members respect the work of teachers as difficult and essential, elevating the profession to the levels it has so long deserved. A post-pandemic school could be a place that champions from inside the system ways in which it could redistribute opportunities to support all students equitably. A post-pandemic school could be a place in which parents are invited, encouraged, and supported as they engage with the teacher in their students' learning. And, finally, a post-pandemic school could be a learning environment in which the human connection is championed above all else in the process of learning.

It remains to be seen how Education emerges on the other side of the pandemic. A return to the status quo seems to be a missed opportunity and a return to a situation in which a single spark could reignite the burn. As educators and community members who rely on the work of educators, let's take the lessons learned from the pandemic to foster our superbloom.

CHAPTER 13

A Transformative and Emancipatory Vision of Scientific Literacy

BY AIDIN AMIRSHOKOOHI AND
MAHSA KAZEMPOUR

In *Let Us Dream*, Pope Francis urges us to "have the courage to change" by "seeing clearly, choosing well, and acting right" so that we, as a global community, may "emerge from the crisis better than before" and "rescue our society, our economy, and our planet." The Pope emphasizes the significance of human ingenuity in the face of crises: "That's the genius in the human story: there's always a way to escape destruction. Where humankind has to act is precisely there, in the threat itself; that's where the door opens."[1]

The COVID-19 pandemic has resulted in an unprecedented focus on the relevance of science to everyday life and simultaneously brought to light the inequities and inadequacies of our education system, particularly with respect to science and STEM (Science, Technology, Engineering, Mathematics) education. Since the beginning of the pandemic, science and the related fields of mathematics, technology, and engineering have been at the forefront of daily conversations, news, debates, social media coverage, and policy decisions regarding protective face coverings, physical distancing, quarantines, transmission of the virus, and the spread of infection, as well as approaches to treatment and prevention of COVID-19. Throughout this time, the public has witnessed a constant tension between opinion and evidence, and we were inundated with a mass spread of misinformation, dubbed an "infodemic" by the World Health Organization (WHO). The COVID-19 crisis has underscored the significance of improving our education system, particularly with respect to science education, to allow individuals and societies to be able to discern between reliable information and misinformation and engage in informed and responsible decision making and policy formulation.

In response to the recent crisis, UNESCO released nine ideas or calls for action for post-COVID pandemic education. Among them was one focusing on the significance of science education: "Ensure scientific literacy within the curriculum. This is the right time for deep reflection on curriculum, particularly as we struggle against the denial of scientific knowledge and actively fight misinformation."[2] The pandemic has forced us, as a global community, to take action on numerous fronts, including the improvement of future generations' education, particularly in terms of science, and by extension STEM, education. In the face of global crises, including climate change and mass environmental destruction, COVID-19, war and conflict, hunger, and more, it is critical that we ponder and reassess the real purpose and intended goals of education. As teachers, teacher educators, education policy makers, and educational stakeholders, we must heed the urgent call for action and collectively strive to enhance the state of science and STEM education and prioritize scientific literacy.

The term "scientific literacy" has been part of the science education lexicon since the 1950s and became particularly important as the central goal of science education was articulated in various educational reform documents originating in the 1990s.[3] Despite its ubiquitous use in science education, there is a lack of a universally accepted definition of scientific literacy.[4] Liliana Valladares argues that the traditional definition of scientific literacy, identified as Vision-I, focuses mainly on learning scientific content and processes and has been linked to the preparation of future scientists. Vision-II of scientific literacy, identified as the perspective of "science for all," emphasizes the socio-cultural contexts and dimensions of science and the importance of understanding the application and value of science in life and society.[5]

Finally, Vision-III of scientific literacy extends beyond the social contextualization of science and focuses on meeting complex global challenges and the transformation of society (social, political, cultural, economic, and environmental) through informed decision making, public discourse, social engagement, and democratic participation, as well as individual and collective action and agency.[6] This particular vision of literacy is aligned with Paul Freire's critical pedagogy which argues that education should be humanistic and serve as a means of awakening the critical consciousness and transforming oppressive and inequitable systems.[7] According to Sjöström and Eilks, Vision-III is "a politicized vision of science education aiming at dialogical emancipation, critical global citizenship, and socio-ecojustice," in which "controversial, relevant, and authentic socio-scientific issues, e.g. from the sustainability debate, shall become the drivers for the curriculum."[8]

This transformative vision of scientific literacy aligns perfectly with the Science, Technology, Society (STS) framework of science education that was first advocated more than three decades ago and continues to be emphasized in important science education documents and initiatives such as the *Framework for K–12 Science Education* and *The Next Generation Science Standards.*[9] The STS framework focuses on the interdependence of science, technology, and society, which is highlighted in the following excerpts from the *Framework for K–12 Science Education:*

> *Not only do science and engineering affect society; society's decisions (whether made through market forces or political processes) influence the work of scientists and engineers. These decisions sometimes establish goals and priorities for improving or replacing technologies; at other times they set limits, such as in regulating the extraction of raw materials or in setting allowable levels of pollution from mining, farming, and industry.*

> *Together, advances in science, engineering, and technology can have—and indeed have had—profound effects on human society, in such areas as agriculture, transportation, health care, and communication, and on the natural envi-*

ronment. Each system can change significantly when new technologies are introduced, with both desired effects and unexpected outcomes.[10]

The STS education framework aims to prepare students to critically understand scientific and technological developments in their cultural, ethical, environmental, economic, political, and social contexts. An STS-based instructional approach is inherently interdisciplinary and involves active engagement and immersion of students in exploring real-world issues, such as deforestation, climate change, nuclear energy, genetic engineering, and disease control, that are grounded in science and technology.[11] The STS approach to teaching and learning emphasizes informed decision-making, ethical reflection and judgment, independent thinking, social action, transformation, and empowerment.[12]

The implementation and adoption of an STS-based approach to science education, with a focus on Vision-III transformative scientific literacy, depends on several factors including the preparation of current and future teachers to become agents of change who in turn educate their students to serve as agents of change in their local and global communities. Teacher education programs and courses must equip teachers with deep and critical understanding of science and STS issues as well as enhance their perceptions and attitudes toward science and teaching science in a socially contextualized and transformative manner.

In *Let Us Dream*, Pope Francis reminds us that our response to the COVID-19 pandemic and the less visible, yet significant global crises facing humanity, such as environmental degradation; social, environmental, and economic injustice and inequality; and human rights violations must "begin with an integral ecology, an ecology that takes seriously the cultural and ethical deterioration that goes hand in hand with our ecological crisis."[13] As the pope suggests, to fulfill our desire to reimagine our world and not return to the previous global state, we must "see clearly" through the adoption of a different lens, "choose well," and "act right."[14] In order to achieve a sustainable future and more just and equitable societies, we must "dare to dream" and pursue a global commitment to a radical, transformative, and emancipatory vision of scientific learning that "recovers Freirean approaches and deepens the educational engagement to change oppression and alienation, humanizing school science and transforming the inequitable social reality of the globalized world."[15]

CHAPTER 14

Pope Francis on Person-Centered Education

BY KEVIN NADOLSKI

At the height of the COVID-19 pandemic, Pope Francis released an encyclical letter, *Fratelli Tutti*, for believers to consider the call to and urgency of human fraternity and social friendship, defining the latter as "a love capable of transcending borders" that "makes true universal openness possible."[1] Such an urgent beckoning resounds in any season, and it echoes thunderously in a time of pandemic. The October 4, 2020 publication, which coincided with the feast day of his papal patron saint, Francis of Assisi, preceded the approval and widespread usage of the vaccine that has saved countless lives. Yet, neither the pope's letter nor subsequent inoculations have spared people anxiety, pain, suffering, and injustice.

Children and youth, while infected by the virus in substantially fewer numbers, still experience the ravages of the disease, whether in or out of school. Two statistics may startle the most sober observer. First, more than 140,000 youth have lost a parent or primary caregiver to COVID-19. Most of these young people are from racial and ethnic minorities.[2] Second, growing evidence suggests that the pandemic has widened pre-existing educational disparities in learners' math and reading abilities and access to technology, especially for students of color.[3]

Perhaps the pope's call for love and openness is as necessary as a vaccine during a pandemic, and schools may be the necessary and best place to provide them for our youth. With great timeliness, Pope Francis offers wisdom on education for learning, regardless of one's faith tradition or school context. His consistent message on education acclaims a foundation that is both human and social. A brief consideration of each is in order.

HUMAN

The impact of Pope Francis' papacy is not limited to his own writings. The efforts of his collaborators in his leadership team of the curia reflect well his spirit, message, and—most especially—vision for the church and world. A little known but important document from his Congregation for Catholic Education marks a paradigm shift in a Catholic understanding of education. *Educating to Fraternal Humanism* asserts that the human person is the center of education. Implicit here is that the person, not the curriculum—be it religious or secular, not the economic market that a student will enter, and not a vocational trade or professional service that the graduate will serve; it is the person who is the center and focus of education. The congregation's call for humanizing education is "putting the person at the center of education, in a framework of relationships that make up a living community, which is interdependent and bound to a common destiny."[4]

The release of *Educating to Fraternal Humanism* was to mark the fiftieth anniversary of another papal encyclical, *Populorum Progressio,* where Pope Paul VI in 1967 aligned world peace with human development, which is facilitated and advanced uniquely by education: "Development is the new name for peace."[5] The tenets of *Educating to Fraternal Humanism* foreshadow the foundational elements of the pandemic document *Fratelli Tutti.* In addition to humanizing education, the document calls for a culture of dialogue, globalizing hope, cooperation networks, and true inclusion. With almost prophetic prescience, its definition of dialogue presents both a challenge and roadmap for our society presently debating, often with acrimony and ideological rigidity, issues such as whether to be vaccinated, use a face covering, or limit participation in large social events. True dialogue has ethical requirements, including "freedom and equality," where "participants…must be free from their contingent interests and must be prepared to recognize the dignity of all parties."[6] We can only imagine the wisdom and peace that would bless us if we, our friends and family members, church and political leaders, and media personalities took a cue from this understanding of dialogue.

Moreover, Pope Francis expanded and amplified the five human-centered tenets of this education office in his 2020 address to a global meeting of educators, where he outlined seven tasks to "create harmony" and respond to "situations of loneliness and uncertainty about the future that affect young people and generate depression, addiction, aggressiveness, verbal hatred and bullying."

1. *To make human persons in their value and dignity the center of every educational program, both formal and informal, in order to foster their distinctiveness, beauty and uniqueness, and their capacity for relationship with others and with the world around them, while at the same time teaching them to reject lifestyles that encourage the spread of the throwaway culture.*

2. *To listen to the voices of children and young people to whom we pass on values and knowledge, in order to build together a future of justice, peace and a dignified life for every person.*

3. *To encourage the full participation of girls and young women in education.*

4. *To see in the family the first and essential place of education.*

5. *To educate and be educated on the need for acceptance and in particular openness to the most vulnerable and marginalized.*

6. *To be committed to finding new ways of understanding the economy, politics, growth and progress that can truly stand at the service of the human person and the entire human family, within the context of an integral ecology.*

7. *To safeguard and cultivate our common home, pro-
    tecting it from the exploitation of its resources, and to
    adopt a more sober lifestyle marked by the use of renew-
    able energy sources and respect for the natural and
    human environment, in accordance with the principles
    of subsidiarity, solidarity and a circular economy.*[7]

SOCIAL

Pope Francis' insistence on the primacy of the social order over any
sort of individualized approach to life cannot be clearer. Again, he said
in *Fratelli Tutti*, in reference to the pandemic: "No one is saved alone;
we can only be saved together."[8] What's more, his aforementioned seven
essential educational tasks to address the challenges, ailments, and
dysfunctions plaguing today's youth are explicitly social in nature. At
every turn, "Francis is calling all people to wake up from their focus on
and infatuation with self to see the world relationally."[9] Relatedly, he
also warns against a "'local' narcissism unrelated to a healthy love of
one's own people and culture,...born of a certain insecurity and fear of
the other that leads to rejection and the desire to erect walls for self-
defense."[10] Recalling his definition of social friendship, believers can
come to understand that a true disciple can only love by transcending
borders, walls, and even collectively narcissistic egos.

Likewise, the definition of humanizing education, articulated in
Educating to Fraternal Humanism, requires a "framework of relationships that make up a living community."[11] This social dynamism that
both forms and informs the education of a young person from early
childhood to the tertiary levels of schooling is a complex web of relationships where one experiences learning, trust, compassion, and love. Yes,
no one can be saved alone, and no one can truly learn alone, if human,
loving relationships are absent. Or, as revealed in Genesis, all know: "It
is not good for the man to be alone" (Genesis 2:18). Sadly then, for more
than 140,000 young people to have lost their parents and primary caregivers is not merely a matter of sadness; it is an egregious violation of
social justice that beckons a society to respond with interventions that
illustrate the responsibility held for the education of children.

However, the greatest affirmation of the essential social dimension of education is his insistence on the social character of human life itself, as asserted in the encyclical on care for creation, *Laudato Si*, which he deliberately "added to the body of the Church's social teaching."[12] Here, he declares—repeatedly—that "everything is interconnected."[13] For this reason, education and schooling have reciprocal implications for ethical responses to climate change and environmental degradation, for efforts to advance social justice, and for calls to end poverty, racism, and sexism—all evident in the pope's seven educational tasks.

Such an interrelated and integrated approach to humanity impacts a parallel framework of human relationships for education, as seen in *Educating for Fraternal Humanism*. Yet, the clarity around this approach in *Laudato Si* highlights the far-reaching implications of integral ecology, which he raises to a guiding Gospel ethic that is indispensable for all believers:

> Since everything is closely interrelated, and today's problems call for a vision capable of taking into account every aspect of the global crisis, I suggest that we now consider some elements of an integral ecology, one which clearly respects its human and social dimensions.[14]

Here, the pope

> suggests that there is an intimate relationship with creation and that the redemption of the person and the universe are inextricably linked. All things are connected in a web of life. It is spirituality of relationship that calls us to real human development.[15]

This ethic of integral ecology has direct implications for education in general and for ecological education in particular. The latter, as a holistic model, is proposed by Pope Francis with the goal of "reestablishing harmony with nature, with others, and with God."[16] The pope is quick to place the responsibility for this instruction and formation before all baptized people: "All Christian communities have an important role to play in ecological education."[17]

CONCLUSION: POPE FRANCIS AND
ST. FRANCIS DE SALES

Returning to the young people whose lives and stories stand vulnerably behind the statistics presented at the opening of this chapter, baptized people could easily grow sad or angry. But, because of the demands of the social implications of baptism, might disciples feel responsible for those students who—due to the injustices emerging from the pandemic—have lost a parent or caregiver and for those students whose math and reading skills and access to technology have plummeted?

Pope Francis' reflection in *Fratelli Tutti* on the parable of the Good Samaritan suggests a strong *Yes* in response to this question. Bemused by why it took so long for the church to condemn slavery and other violence and injustices, the pope states clearly: "Today, with our developed spirituality and theology, we have no excuses."[18] His appeal to spirituality, which is the "personal relationship of a human being with God, along with all the attitudes and modes of expression that this relationship includes,"[19] prompts a new question: What attitudes and modes of expression can move an educational context to address the needs of students emerging from the pandemic? Two stand as primary after a consideration of the contributions of Pope Francis: kindness and Christian humanism, which rest in the nucleus of the legacy of St. Francis de Sales.

"Recovering Kindness" is a unique section of *Fratelli Tutti*. Penned during the pandemic, this consideration names "consumerist individualism" as leading to "great injustice" and advances kindness as an antidote to such social illness.[20] A spirituality grounded in kindness, in the words of the pope, "transforms lifestyles, relationships, and the ways ideas are discussed and compared. Kindness facilitates the quest for consensus; it opens new paths where hostility and conflict would burn all bridges."[21]

Similarly, Christian humanism, a philosophical approach that acclaims the human person as created and loved by God, is a "dynamic, integrative process that is brought about through the engagement of the whole person."[22] Foundational to *Educating for Fraternal Humanism* and *Fratelli Tutti* is the call to encounter the human person: "I have frequently called for the growth of a culture of encounter capable of transcending our differences and divisions.... Each of us can learn something from others.... This also means finding ways to include those on the peripheries of life."[23]

St. Francis de Sales, a seventeenth-century French bishop and doctor of the church famous for his spiritual writings, is still acclaimed for his Christian humanism and the optimistic view of the human person in his writings. Additionally, his spirituality—developed in concert with St. Jane de Chantal—is renowned for the centrality of kindness: "Kindness was the keynote of St. Francis de Sales."[24]

The nexus between the pope and the saint who share a name also includes their approach to the world and the church. De Sales, known as the gentleman saint, engaged his world and church, in a time replete with violence, with a "new tenderness and a new a gentleness."[25] Similarly, Pope Francis envisions the church as field hospital, messy by nature, and encounters it with a Salesian tenderness and gentleness. While the pope's name refers to the Francis from Assisi, Francis de Sales' spirituality and writings provide a wealth of support to the pontiff's educational perspective that hails kindness and humanity as chief means to advancing the development of young people through the experience of superior learning that must occur in all schools.

DeSales University Faculty

Aidin Amirshokoohi, PhD
ASSOCIATE PROFESSOR

Dr. Aidin Amirshokoohi is an Associate Professor of STEM Education in the Department of Education. He earned his teaching certification and Master of Arts in Teaching at the University of Iowa and pursued his PhD in science and environmental education at Indiana University Bloomington.

At DeSales University, he is responsible for teaching a variety of courses each year including Science Methods, Mathematics Content and Method, Advanced Designing Instructions, Technology for Educators, STEM in the Elementary Classroom, and the graduate capstone research course. He also serves as the Secondary Education Program Advisor for students seeking secondary teaching certification in areas of science, math, history, English, etc.

For his chapter in this volume, Dr. Amirshokoohi collaborated with Dr. Mahsa Kazempour, an associate professor of science education at Penn State Berks. Their shared research interests include the impact of inquiry-based teaching and learning, Environmental Education, and Science, Technology, Society (STS)—an interdisciplinary field and learning approach that focuses on teaching science in the context of controversial socio-scientific issues and involves applying K–12 STEM concepts to real-world societal situations.

Katrin L. Blamey, PhD
ASSOCIATE PROFESSOR, EDUCATION DEPARTMENT CHAIR,
DIRECTOR OF MED PROGRAMS

Dr. Blamey has experience teaching and researching in early childhood educational settings, including Head Start. She has been a teacher educator for many years.

Her fields of primary interest include developmentally appropriate teaching practices, vocabulary instruction, literacy for struggling readers, and elementary education methods.

At DeSales University, she is chair of the education department and coordinator of the Early Childhood and Elementary Education Program. She teaches undergraduate and graduate courses in Early Childhood Foundations, Literacy Methods, Reading Assessment, and Children's Literature.

Stephen J. Carp, PT, PhD
ASSISTANT PROFESSOR

Dr. Stephen Carp has been an assistant professor in the Doctor of Physical Therapy program at DeSales University since 2016. He received Bachelor and Master of Science degrees in physical therapy and a PhD in motor control from Temple University.

Dr. Carp has over thirty years of clinical experience in many arenas of physical therapy, including acute care, outpatient, wound care, skilled nursing, and acute medical rehabilitation. He is an ABPTS board certified geriatric specialist. In addition to his clinical work, Dr. Carp has held numerous administrative and consultative positions in hospitals, including vice-president of quality, vice-president of performance improvement, and interim CEO.

Dr. Carp's primary teaching responsibilities in the curriculum include Differential Diagnosis and Intervention—Geriatrics, Differential Diagnosis and Intervention—Cardiopulmonary, Professional Development 3, Clinical Reasoning 4, Clinical Medicine 3—Special Populations, Business and Management Issues, and Special Topics 2—Global Health.

In addition to his teaching responsibilities, Dr. Carp is a faculty mentor for student research projects in PT Research 1–4. He pursues three research lines: non-academic intelligence metrics related to graduate admissions, the effectiveness of non-government support for the poor, and the effect of exercise on cognitive and fall-risk metrics in persons with Alzheimer's disease. He has authored over fifteen publications and has published three textbooks, most recently *Foundations: An Introduction to Physical Therapy*, published in January of 2019 by Thieme.

Dr. Carp and his wife, Diane, have three wonderful children and two grandchildren. He enjoys spending his free time running, gardening, woodworking, and providing service to the poor through the Society of Saint Vincent de Paul.

Christopher R. Cocozza, CPA, JD, LLM
PROFESSOR, DIVISION HEAD

Professor Cocozza is an attorney with a JD from Fordham University School of Law and an LLM in taxation from New York University School of Law and is licensed to practice law in both New Jersey and New York. He has a BS in accounting from Fordham University College of Business Administration and is a licensed CPA in Pennsylvania.

He has been a DeSales University faculty member for over twenty years and department chair/division head for fourteen years in the Division of Business. He teaches Federal Income Taxation, Regulation and the Legal Environment of Business Law at the undergraduate level. He teaches Advanced Law and Taxation in the

MBA program. He has several years of industry experience in the area of taxation at Deloitte, LLP and the Lexis Publishing Group. He has published papers in the areas of taxation and retirement planning in *America*, *The Pennsylvania CPA Journal*, and *The Journal of Financial Planning*.

Professor Cocozza is the co-mentor of the Accounting and Finance Club and the Volunteer Income Tax Assistance (VITA) Program. The VITA Program has been recognized by the IRS and Commonwealth of Pennsylvania for its volunteer work, and the program has been featured in *The Morning Call*, on *Service Electric News*, on radio station WAEB, and on Lehigh Valley PBS. During the past twenty years, business students have completed over 5,000 tax returns for more than 2,500 Lehigh Valley taxpayers. These services have resulted in taxpayer compliance savings of over $250,000 and have provided students with invaluable life experience.

Professor Cocozza is happily married to his wife, Danielle, and they have three wonderful children: Lauren, Kristen, and Michael.

Elisabeth Felten, CPA, CGMA
ASSISTANT PROFESSOR

Elisabeth Felten is an assistant professor in the Division of Business, where she teaches undergraduate and MBA-level classes in accounting. Prior to joining DeSales, she taught in the business schools at the University of Iowa and University of Minnesota.

She earned her MBA from the University of Iowa, Tippie College of Business and her BSBA in Accounting from American University. She holds CPA licenses in Maryland, New Jersey, and Pennsylvania and is a Chartered Global Management Accountant (CGMA). Elisabeth is a member of the American Institute of CPAs and has earned their certificates in Not-for-Profit accounting and Data Analytics.

Professor Felten teaches financial, managerial, governmental, and not-for-profit accounting, data analytics for accounting and finance majors, and general business courses, including new ventures and international business.

When not on campus, Elisabeth serves on a panel that trains judges and court officials on autism. She also coaches special needs soccer in Upper Township, NJ.

The Rev. James Greenfield, OSFS, EdD
PRESIDENT

Father James Greenfield, OSFS, a priest with the Oblates of St. Francis de Sales, was born and raised in Philadelphia, Pennsylvania. A graduate of Allentown College of St. Francis de Sales, DeSales School of Theology, and The George Washington University, Fr. Jim holds degrees in politics, divinity, and counseling psychology. He also completed an EdD from The George Washington University in human development.

Fr. Jim has taught at Salesianum School, The George Washington University, Washington Theological Union, and DeSales University. For the Oblates, he served as vocation director, provincial councilor, director of seminary formation, president of the conference of major superiors of men, and provincial. Additionally, he serves on the boards of numerous non-profit and charitable organizations, and he leads parish missions and diocesan retreats for parishioners in several dioceses.

Tahereh Alavi Hojjat, PhD
PROFESSOR, CHAIR OF ECONOMICS

Tahereh Alavi Hojjat is professor and Chair of Economics at DeSales University. Dr. Hojjat received her bachelor's degree from Tehran University, Iran, her master's degree from the American University, Washington, DC, and her PhD from Lehigh University in Bethlehem, Pennsylvania. She is past recipient of the Teaching Excellence Award by the Eastern Council of Business Schools and Programs (ECBSP). She has received grants from the Center for Advancing Partnership in Education (CAPE) for Global Collaborative Faculty Projects and Lehigh Valley Association of Independent Colleges (LVAIC) for the College Admission Mentoring Program (CAMP).

She has authored several book chapters and articles in peer-reviewed journals of business and social sciences. She has served as an advisory board member of Houghton-Mifflin Publishing and McGraw Hill companies and currently serves as an Academic Advisory Board Member for Taking Sides: Clashing Views on Global Issues, and the *Journal of Asian Finance, Economics and Business* (*JAFEB*). The second edition of her book *The Economics of Obesity: Poverty, Income Inequality and Health*, was published by Springer in 2021.

Sue Y. McGorry, PhD
PROFESSOR, ASSISTANT PROVOST

Sue McGorry is Assistant Provost for Assessment, Curriculum and Student Success and Professor of Business at DeSales University. Prior to her appointment at DeSales, McGorry held positions with Chase Manhattan Bank, AT&T, and UNESCO in France. Her professional memberships include the American Marketing Association (faculty advisor for the DeSales chapter), the Atlantic Marketing Association, the Marketing Science Institute, and the Association of Collegiate Marketing Educators.

Professor McGorry teaches Marketing Research and Analytics, Data Mining, and Healthcare Marketing. She has managed numerous service learning initiatives at DeSales University in both undergraduate and graduate programs with organizations like Girls on the Run, the United Way, and Special Olympics. McGorry's research interests include service quality in education and healthcare, measurement, service learning, and technology in marketing and education.

McGorry serves on the board of the Eastern Pennsylvania Down Syndrome Center and Lehigh Valley Hospital's Institutional Review Board and she is a peer evaluator for the Middle States Commission on Higher Education. She has authored a variety of articles, presentations, and publications with the American Marketing Association, the Atlantic Marketing Association, and the Online Learning Consortium. McGorry earned the MBA and PhD in Marketing and Applied Research from Lehigh University and has completed post-doctoral work at the Massachusetts Institute of Technology. She is most proud of her three daughters Meghan, Shannon, and Molly and has served as cross country and track and field coach as well as stage crew!

Bobbie Morici, MSPAS, PA-C, DFAAPA
ASSISTANT PROFESSOR, ASSISTANT PROGRAM DIRECTOR, CLINICAL COORDINATOR

Bobbie Morici has been an NCCPA certified physician assistant since 2005. She completed her bachelor's degree from Pennsylvania State University in nutrition science and her master's degree in physician assistant studies from DeSales University. She has practiced in internal medicine at Lehigh Valley Hospital and Health Network since graduation.

She has managed patients in the inpatient, outpatient, and nursing home settings. Bobbie joined the DeSales PA Program in July 2012 as a clinical coordinator and was named director of clinical education in January 2014. She is a member of the Physician Assistant Education Association, American Academy of Physician Assistants, and Pennsylvania Society of Physician Assistants. She has presented professionally on the local and national levels and has been published in the *Journal of the American Academy of Physician Assistants* and the *Journal of Physician Assistant Education.*

The Rev. Kevin Nadolski, OSFS, PhD
ASSISTANT PROFESSOR, VICE PRESIDENT FOR MISSION

Father Kevin Nadolski, OSFS, a priest with the Oblates of St. Francis de Sales, was born and raised in Philadelphia, Pennsylvania. A graduate of Temple University, Catholic University of America, and DeSales School of Theology, Fr. Kevin holds degrees in journalism, divinity, and education administration. He also holds a PhD from Fordham University in administration and supervision of education.

Fr. Kevin has worked as a teacher and principal in Catholic high schools and also served as vocation director, director of the seminary, director of development and communications, and assistant provincial for the Oblates in Wilmington, Delaware. He presently serves at DeSales University as vice president for mission and assistant professor of education.

Jacqueline M. Ochsenreither, DNP, CRNP, PPCNP-BC
ASSISTANT PROFESSOR; DIRECTOR, DOCTOR OF NURSING PRACTICE PROGRAM

Dr. Jacqueline Ochsenreither is an Assistant Professor of Nursing and Director of the Doctor of Nursing Practice Program at DeSales University. She has been a pediatric critical-care nurse practitioner for more than twenty-six years. She has cared for infants, children, and adolescents in a variety of pediatric nursing roles at St. Christopher's Hospital for Children, including adolescent medicine, cardiac intensive care, emergency medicine, transport team, and cardiac catheterization.

She has experience practicing as an advanced practice nurse at the Children's Hospital of Philadelphia in pediatric pain management, cardiac-intensive care, lung and heart/lung transplant, and as a pediatric hospitalist at Doylestown Hospital. She has teaching experience at the doctoral, graduate, and undergraduate levels at DeSales University, the University of Pennsylvania Graduate School of Nursing, and Thomas Jefferson University School of Nursing. She has precepted both didactically and clinically for many years, focusing on pediatric acute and critical-care. She is board-certified and serves as a reviewer for Pediatric Nursing.

Dr. Ochsenreither graduated with her BSN from Allentown College of St. Francis de Sales in 1985. She graduated from the University of Pennsylvania Graduate School of Nursing with her MSN and CRNP in pediatric critical-care in 1994 and received her Doctor of Nursing Practice degree from DeSales University in Clinical Leadership in 2015.

Karen A. Peterson, RN, PMHCNS-BC, PMHNP-BC
ASSISTANT PROFESSOR, DIRECTOR OF THE ACCESS BSN PROGRAM

Karen Peterson is an assistant professor in the Division of Nursing and has taught the Mental Health Nursing course for over ten years. She is a certified psychiatric clinical nurse specialist and psychiatric-mental health nurse practitioner. She has served in a variety of primary care roles. Her experience includes practice in a clinical specialist role as well as director of a psychiatric unit. Ms. Peterson continues in clinical practice as a nurse practitioner as well as providing education and consultation at Lehigh Valley Hospital.

Ms. Peterson is responsible for teaching the traditional day Mental Health Nursing courses as well as teaching in the Clinical Nurse Specialist and Psychiatric Mental Health Nurse Practitioner programs. In addition, she teaches the Capstone Project Course in the RN-BSN program. She is currently the director for the ACCESS Nursing Program at DeSales University.

Ms. Peterson received her nursing diploma from Good Samaritan Hospital School of Nursing in Portland, Oregon. She then completed her BSN at George Mason University in Fairfax, Virginia. She completed her MSN at Rutgers University with a specialty of psychiatric/mental health nursing. In January 2018, she completed the Post-Graduate Certificate Program as a psychiatric nurse practitioner at DeSales University.

Brennan C. Pursell, MBA, PhD
ASSOCIATE PROFESSOR, DIRECTOR OF THE CENTER FOR DATA ANALYTICS

Dr. Brennan Pursell, associate professor of business and director of the Center for Data Analytics at DeSales University, teaches courses in data analytics, artificial intelligence (AI), and management in the undergraduate and graduate programs.

His recent book, *Outsmarting AI: Power, Profit, and Leadership in the Age of Machines* (Rowman & Littlefield, 2020), destroys widespread myths about artificial intelligence, clarifies the technology's capabilities and limitations across economic sectors, and shows how to implement it profitably, ethically, and in accordance with the law.

A dedicated life-long learner, he works on data analytics, coding, and AI skill development and projects every day. The world is changing, now faster than ever. More and more digitized data about people and how they live and work are being captured, collected, stored, analyzed, and put to use. AI is expanding the range of automated tasks that machines can take over from humans. We have to learn to use AI instead of letting it use us!

Outside of academia, Brennan has worked as a management consultant for firms large and small, from multinational corporations to niche technology firms and startups. He recently participated in a project to educate and prepare the state courts of the USA to defend themselves against digital mis- and disinformation, cyber-attacks, and AI deepfakes.

In his twenty-eight-year academic career, he first trained as an historian (AB Stanford 1990, PhD Harvard 2000) and researched, taught, and published four books and dozens of articles about topics in modern European history. He has appeared on *CNN, EWTN,* and other television stations, in addition to eighty radio outlets, and in interviews with over a dozen major American newspapers. He completed an MBA degree at DeSales University in 2014.

Amy K. S. Scott, PhD
ASSOCIATE PROFESSOR

Dr. Scott received her BA from Penn State and MBA and PhD from Lehigh University. Her doctoral studies in economics included concentrations in public finance and international economics.

Prior to coming to the Division of Business at DeSales, Dr. Scott taught at both Lehigh University and Lafayette College. She teaches courses in economics and finance at both the undergraduate and graduate levels. Undergraduate courses taught include Economics of Public Issues, Principles of Macroeconomics, Principles of Microeconomics, and Personal Finance. In the MBA program, she teaches Economics and Managerial Finance.

Her articles have appeared in several journals, including *Thunderbird International Business Review, Sport Management International Journal, Journal of Sport and Tourism,* and *International Economic Journal.* Her current research includes the regional economic impact of sporting events. Past projects include the 2009 US Women's Open Golf Championship and the Lehigh Valley Marathon for Via 2010–2018.

She co-authored a 2020 textbook with DeSales associate professor Bradley Barnhorst, CFA, for Flat World Knowledge entitled *Managerial Finance,* with the latest edition being published in March 2021.

Deborah Whittaker, EdD, MSN, RN, RNC-MNN
ASSOCIATE PROFESSOR, CHAIR OF UNDERGRADUATE
NURSING PROGRAMS

Dr. Deborah Whittaker is an associate professor of clinical nursing in the Division of Nursing. Additionally, Dr. Whittaker is the Chair of Undergraduate Nursing Programs. She has a background in a variety of patient care settings, including hospitals and home health. Her clinical experience includes obstetrics, newborn, pediatrics, orthopedics, and neurology as well as management experience in pediatric endocrinology. Dr. Whittaker is certified in Maternal Newborn Nursing.

Dr. Whittaker teaches in both the undergraduate and graduate nursing programs. Her undergraduate teaching responsibilities have included Fundamentals of Nursing, Nursing of the Childbearing Family, Concepts of Professional Nursing, Senior Integrating Seminar, and Senior Internship. On the graduate level, teaching responsibilities include Clinical Prevention in Population Health. Dr. Whittaker enjoys teaching in the traditional classroom as well as online, in the laboratory, and in the clinical setting.

Dr. Whittaker received her BSN with academic distinction from the State University of New York at Binghamton, MSN in nursing education with specialization in women's health from DeSales University, and her EdD in organizational leadership with an emphasis in higher education from Grand Canyon University, Arizona. Dr. Whittaker is the chair of the nursing undergraduate admissions and standards committee, the outcomes assessment committee, as well as an active participant on several university committees. She is a member of Sigma Theta Tau International, Mu Omicron Chapter. In her leisure time, Dr. Whittaker enjoys outdoor activities with her family, church, and spending time with friends.

FOREWORD

1   E. O. Wilson, *Consilience: The Unity of Knowledge* (New York: Vintage, 1999), 294.

INTRODUCTION: YES, FRANCIS!

1   Pope Francis and Austen Ivereigh, *Let Us Dream: the path to a better future* (New York: Simon & Schuster, 2020), 105.

CHAPTER 1: MARKET RESET: RESPECT THE CUSTOMER AS A PERSON

1   "Pope Francis: Life Is a Constant Call to Go Forth," *Vatican News*, November 3, 2018. https://www.vaticannews.va/en/pope/news/2018-11/pope-homily-mass-deceased-cardinals-bishops.html

CHAPTER 2: CREATE A MORE EQUITABLE TAX STRUCTURE

1   See "Income Inequality in the United States," *Inequality.org*. https://inequality.org/facts/income-inequality/
2   K. Taylor, "A chart shows how Jeff Bezos's net worth exploded by $75 billion in 2020, reaching $188 billion before he stepped down as Amazon's CEO," *Business Insider*, February 2, 2021. https://www.businessinsider.com/amazon-ceo-jeff-bezos-net-worth-explodes-in-2020-chart-2020-12
3   J. Eisinger, J. Ernsthausen, and P. Kiel, "The secret IRS files: Trove of never-before-seen records reveal how the wealthiest avoid income taxation," *ProPublica*, June 8, 2021. https://www.propublica.org/article/the-secret-irs-files-trove-of-never-before-seen-records-reveal-how-the-wealthiest-avoid-income-tax
4   Eisinger, Ernsthausen, and Kiel.
5   See *JP Morgan Chase 2020 Annual Report*. https://www.jpmorganchase.com/content/dam/jpmc/jpmorgan-chase-and-co/investor-relations/documents/annualreport-2020.pdf
6   Eisinger, Ernsthausen, and Kiel.
7   E. Saez and G. Zucman, "How to Get $1 Trillion from 1000 Billionaires: Tax their Gains Now," *University of California Berkeley*, April 14, 2021. https://eml.berkeley.edu/~saez/SZ21-billionaire-tax.pdf

CHAPTER 3: THE FUTURE OF WORK

1   K. Engemann, "How has the COVID-19 pandemic affected the U.S. labor market?" *Federal Reserve Bank of St. Louis*, October 14, 2020. https://www.stlouisfed.org/open-vault/2020/october/how-covid19-pandemic-has-affected-labor-market

2   K. Terrell, "8 Occupations hit hardest by the pandemic," *AARP*, January 21, 2020. https://www.aarp.org/work/job-search/info-2020/job-losses-during-covid.html

3   E. Gould and M. Kassa, "Low-wage, low-hour workers were hit hardest in the COVID-19 recession," *Economic Policy Institute*, May 20, 2021. https://www.epi.org/publication/swa-2020-employment-report/

4   Gould and Kassa, note 3.

5   Engemann.

6   Tableau Research, "Fall 2020 Undergraduate enrollment revised downward as more colleges report to the Clearinghouse." https://public.tableau.com/app/profile/researchcenter/viz/Fall20203asofOct_22/Fall2020EnrollmentNo_3

7   K. Field, "The Missing Men: The gender gap among college students only worsened during the pandemic. Is it a problem colleges are willing to tackle?" *The Chronicle of Higher Education*, July 1, 2021. https://www.chronicle.com/article/the-missing-men?utm_source=Iterable&utm_medium=email&utm_campaign=campaign_2560024_nl_Academe-Today_date_20210708&cid=at&source=ams&sourceId=496848

8   M. Oleschuk, "Gender Equity Considerations for Tenure and Promotion during COVID-19," *Canadian Review of Sociology*, August 11, 2020. https://www.ncbi.nlm.nih.gov/pmc/articles/PMC7436417/

9   O. Shurchkov, "Is COVID-19 turning back the clock on gender equality in academia?" April 23, 2020. https://medium.com/@olga.shurchkov/is-covid-19-turning-back-the-clock-on-gender-equality-in-academia-70c00d6b8ba1. Also see #coronapublicationgap for more resources.

10   Gould and Kassa, note 3.

11   Pope Francis and Austen Ivereigh, *Let Us Dream: the path to a better future* (New York: Simon & Schuster, 2020), 131.

12   Engemann, note 1.

13   E. Porter, "Low-Wage Workers Now Have Options, Which Could Mean a Raise," *New York Times*, July 20, 2021. https://www.nytimes.com/2021/07/20/business/economy/workers-wages-mobility.html

14   Engemann, note 1.

15   "How working-time flexibility affects workers' productivity in a routine job," *IZA Newsroom*, December 4, 2020. https://newsroom.iza.org/en/archive/research/how-working-time-flexibility-affects-workers-productivity-in-a-routine-job/

16   T. George, "Four ways to reduce absenteeism in the workplace," *TPP: Principled Recruitment for Work that Matters*, September 29, 2017. https://www.tpp.co.uk/blog/2017/09/four-ways-to-reduce-absenteeism-in-the-workplace

CHAPTER 4: ECONOMICS OF INCLUSION

1   L. Pier, H. J. Hough, M. Christian, N. Bookman, B. Wilkenfeld, R. Miller, "COVID-19 and the Educational Equity Crisis: Evidence on Learning Loss from the CORE Data Collaborative," *Policy Analysis for California Education*, January 25, 2021. https://edpolicyinca.org/newsroom/covid-19-and-educational-equity-crisis

2   S. Liu and J. Parilla, "How family sustaining jobs can power an inclusive recovery in America's regional economies," *The Brookings Institution*, February 18, 2021. https://www.brookings.edu/essay/how-family-sustaining-jobs-can-power-an-inclusive-recovery-in-americas-cities/?utm_campaign=Brookings%20Brief&utm_medium=email&utm_content=111852064&utm_source=hs_email

3   E. Dorn, B. Hancock, J. Sarakatsannis, and E. Viruleg, "COVID-19 and learning loss—disparities grow and students need help," *McKinsey & Company*, December 8, 2020. https://www.mckinsey.com/industries/public-and-social-sector/our-insights/covid-19-and-learning-loss-disparities-grow-and-students-need-help

4   D. Shipton, et al., "Knowing the goal: an inclusive economy that can address the public health challenges of our time," *Journal of Epidemiology and Community Health*, June 9, 2021. https://jech.bmj.com/content/jech/early/2021/06/21/jech-2020-216070.full.pdf

5   S. Knack and P. Keefer, "Does Social Capital Have an Economic Payoff? A Cross-Country Investigation," *The Quarterly Journal of Economics*, 112(4), (1997), 1251–88.

6   R. Putnam, *Making Democracy Work* (Princeton, NJ: Princeton University Press, 1993).

7   T. Barnes, J. Peck, E. Sheppard, and A. Tickell, *Reading Economic Geography* (Oxford, UK: Blackwell, 2004).

8   J. Jenson and D. Saint-Martin, "New Routes to Social Cohesion? Citizenship and the Social Investment State," *Canadian Journal of Sociology*, 28(1), (2003), 77–99.

9   T. Vinson, "Social Exclusion: The Origins, Meaning, Definition, and Economic Implications of the Concept Social Inclusion/Exclusion," *The Australian Department of Education, Employment, and Workplace Relations*, January 2009. https://vital.voced.edu.au/vital/access/services/Download/ngv:1052/SOURCE2?view=true

10 E. Glaeser, "The Political Economy of Hatred," *The Quarterly Journal of Economics*, 120(1), (2005), 45–86.

11 A. Deaton, *The Great Escape: Health, Wealth, and the Origin of Inequality* (Princeton, NJ: Princeton University Press, 2013), 30.

CHAPTER 5: THE NEW WORK-FROM-HOME WORLD

1   "Kids interrupt dad's live TV interview," CNN. https://www.cnn.com/videos/world/2017/03/10/interview-interrupted-children-newday.cnn

2   S. Usborne, "The expert whose children gatecrashed his TV interview: 'I thought I'd blown it in front of the whole world,'" *The Guardian*, December 20, 2017. https://www.theguardian.com/media/2017/dec/20/robert-kelly-south-korea-bbc-kids-gatecrash-viral-storm

3   A. Hsu, "Millions Of Women Haven't Rejoined The Workforce — And May Not Anytime Soon," *NPR*, June 4, 2021. https://www.npr.org/2021/06/03/1002402802/there-are-complex-forces-keeping-women-from-coming-back-to-work

4   J. Goldstein, "Baby Walks Into Meteorologist Mom's Live TV Shot — and the Internet's in Love: 'You Rocked It!'" *People.* https://people.com/human-interest/baby-walks-into-meteorologist-moms-live-tv-shot-leslie-lopez/

5   J. Barry, "COVID-19 exposes why access to the internet is a human right," *Open Global Rights*, May 26, 2020. https://www.openglobalrights.org/covid-19-exposes-why-access-to-internet-is-human-right/

CHAPTER 6: MORE DATA, PLEASE

1   Tableau Research, May 25, 2021, based on a recent IDC report. https://public.tableau.com/app/profile/tableau.research/viz/DataCultureIDC/DataCultureIDC

2   Quoted in D. Crow, "How mRNA became a vaccine game-changer," *Financial Times Magazine*, May 13, 2021.

3   A. Barbaschow, "Moderna leveraging its 'AI factory' to revolutionise the way diseases are treated," *ZDNet.com*, May 17, 2021. https://www.zdnet.com/article/moderna-leveraging-its-ai-factory-to-revolutionise-the-way-diseases-are-treated/

4   "COVID Data Tracker," Centers for Disease Control and Prevention. https://covid.cdc.gov/covid-data-tracker/#covidnet-hospitalizations-vaccination

5   R. Sharda, D. Delen, and E. Turban, *Analytics, Data Science, & Artificial Intelligence: Systems for Decision Support*, 11th ed. (Hoboken, NJ: Pearson, 2020).

6   B. C. Pursell and J. Walker, *Outsmarting AI: Power, Profit, and Leadership in the Age of Machines* (New York: Rowman & Littlefield, 2020).

7   C. B. Frey, *The Technology Trap: Capital, Labor, and Power in the Age of Automation* (Princeton: Princeton University Press, 2019).

CHAPTER 7: COVID-19 AND THE FUTURE OF HEALTHCARE

1   H. Bauchner, "Medicare and Medicaid, the Affordable Care Act, and US Health Policy," *JAMA* 314(4), (2015), 353–354.

2   K.B. Patterson and T. Runge, "Smallpox and the Native American," *The American Journal of the Medical Sciences* 323(4), (2002), 216-222.

3   J. S. Koopman, J. A. Jacquez, G. W. Welch, C. P. Simon, B. Foxman, S. M. Pollock, K. Lange, et al., "The role of early HIV infection in the spread of HIV through populations," *Journal of Acquired Immune Deficiency Syndromes* 14(3), (2002), 249-258.

4   A. N. Desai and P. Patel, "Stopping the Spread of COVID-19," *JAMA* 323(15), (2002), 1516.

5   "Country Comparisons—Life Expectancy at Birth," CIA World Factbook. https://www.cia.gov/the-world-factbook/field/life-expectancy-at-birth/country-comparison

6   "Health expenditure per capita, 2019," *OECDiLibrary.org.* https://www.oecd-ilibrary.org/sites/ae3016b9-en/1/3/7/2/index.html?itemId=/content/publication/ae3016b9-en&_csp_=ca413da5d44587bc-56446341952c275e&itemIGO=oecd&itemContentType=book

7   E. C. Schneider, D. O. Sarnak, D. Squires, A. Shah, and M. M. Doty, *Mirror Mirror 2017: International Comparison Reflects Flaws and Opportunities for Better U.S. Health Care* (New York: Commonwealth Fund, 2017).

8   Schneider, et al., "Key Findings."

9   H. Alderwick and L. M. Gottlieb, "Meanings and misunderstandings: a social determinants of health lexicon for health care systems," *The Milbank Quarterly* 97(2), (2019), 407.

10 "COVID-19 Weekly Deaths per 100,000 Population by Age, Race/Ethnicity, and Sex, Unites States," Centers for Disease Control and Prevention. https://covid.cdc.gov/covid-data-tracker/#demographicsovertime

11 S. E. Bokemper, G. A. Huber, A. S. Gerber, E. K. James, and S. B. Omer, "Timing of COVID-19 vaccine approval and endorsement by public figures," *Vaccine* 39(5), (2021), 825-829.

12 Editors, "Dying in a leadership vacuum," *New England Journal of Medicine* 383, (2020), 1479-1480.

13 D. Jackson, R. Anders, W. V. Padula, J. Daly, and P. M. Davidson, "Vulnerability of nurse and physicians with COVID-19: Monitoring and surveillance needed," *Journal of Clinical Nursing* 29(19-20), (2020), 3584-3587. M. Z. Gunja and S. R. Collins, "Who are the remaining uninsured, and why do they lack coverage?" *Commonwealth Fund*, August 28, 2019. https://www.commonwealthfund.org/publications/issue-briefs/2019/aug/who-are-remaining-uninsured-and-why-do-they-lack-coverage

14 K. Finegold, A. Conmy, R. C. Chu, A. Bosworth, and B. D. Sommers, "Trends in the U.S. Uninsured Population," *Office of the Assistant Secretary for Planning and Evaluation, U.S. Department of Health and Human Services*, February 11, 2021. https://aspe.hhs.gov/system/files/pdf/265041/trends-in-the-us-uninsured.pdf

CHAPTER 9: ENHANCE THE HUMAN CONNECTION IN MEDICINE

1   NEJM Knowledge+ Team, "Exploring the ACGME Core Competencies (Part 1 of 7)," *NEJM Group*, June 2, 2016. https://knowledgeplus.nejm.org/blog/exploring-acgme-core-competencies/

2   Similar to the ACGME competencies, the competencies for the physician assistant profession originally drafted in 2012 include patient care, interpersonal and communication skills, and professionalism as part of the six competencies. American Academy of Physician Assistants, "Competencies for the Physician Assistant Profession," 2012. https://www.aapa.org/wp-content/uploads/2017/02/PA-Competencies-updated.pdf

3   R. L. Street, L. Liu, N. J. Farber, et al., "Keystrokes, Mouse Clicks, and Gazing at the Computer: How Physician Interaction with the EHR Affects Patient Participation," *Journal of General Internal Medicine* 33 (2018), 423–428. https://doi.org/10.1007/s11606-017-4228-2

4   A. Ramaswamy, M. Yu, S. Drangsholt, E. Ng, P. J. Culligan, P. N. Schlegel, J. C. Hu, "Patient Satisfaction With Telemedicine During the COVID-19 Pandemic: Retrospective Cohort Study," *Journal of Medical Internet Research* 22(9), (2020): e20786. doi: 10.2196/20786

5   Pope Francis and A. Ivereigh, *Let Us Dream: The Path to a Better Future* (New York: Simon & Schuster, 2020), 13.

6   R. D. Zeh, H. P. Santry, C. Monsour, A. A. Sumski, J. Bridges, A. Tsung, T. M. Pawlik, J. M. Cloyd, "Impact of visitor restriction rules on the postoperative experience of COVID-19 negative patients undergoing surgery," *Surgery* 168(5), (2020), 770–776. https://doi.org/10.1016/j.surg.2020.08.010

7   K. Hugelius, N. Harada, M. Marutani, "Consequences of visiting restrictions during the COVID-19 pandemic: An integrative review," *International Journal of Nursing Studies*, 121 (2021). https://doi.org/10.1016/j.ijnurstu.2021.104000

8   Francis and Ivereigh, 137.

CHAPTER 10: INFUSING JOY IN THE YEAR OF THE NURSE

1   "Year of the Nurse and the Midwife 2020," *World Health Organization*. https://www.who.int/campaigns/annual-theme/year-of-the-nurse-and-the-midwife-2020

2   "Sigma Presidential Call to Action 2019-2021," *Sigma Theta Tau International Honor Society of Nursing*. https://www.sigmanursing.org/why-sigma/organizational-leadership/presidential-call-to-action-2019-2021

3   National CNS Competency Task Force, "Clinical Nurse Specialist Core Competencies: Executive Summary 2006–2008," 2010. https://www.nacns.org/wp-content/uploads/2017/01/CNSCoreCompetenciesBroch.pdf

4   J. Kim, J. Park, and S. Shin, "Effectiveness of simulation-based nursing edu-
     cation depending on fidelity: a meta-analysis," *BMC Medical Education* 16
     (2016), 152. https://www.ncbi.nlm.nih.gov/pmc/articles/PMC4877810

5   "Out of the Darkness Walks," *American Foundation for Suicide Prevention.*
     https://supporting.afsp.org/index.cfm?fuseaction=cms.page&id=1370

6   G. d'Ettorre, G. Ceccarelli, L. Santinelli, et al., "Post-Traumatic Stress Symp-
     toms in Healthcare Workers Dealing with the COVID-19 Pandemic: A System-
     atic Review," *International Journal of Environmental Research and Public
     Health* 18(2), (January 2021), 601. https://www.ncbi.nlm.nih.gov/pmc/articles/
     PMC7828167/

7   See Center for Restorative Process: http://www.centerforrestorativeprocess.com/

CHAPTER 11: COVID-19: A MENTAL HEALTH 9/11 FOR COLLEGE STUDENTS

1   P. D. McGorry, R. Purcell, S. Goldstone, and G. P. Amminger, "Age of onset and
     timing of treatment for mental and substance use disorders: Implications for
     preventive intervention strategies and models of care," *Current Opinion in Psy-
     chiatry* 24(4), 2011, 301–306. https://doi.org/10.1097/YCO.0b013e3283477a09

2   S. K. Lipson, E. G. Lattie, and D. Eisenberg, "Increased Rates of Mental Health
     Service Utilization by U.S. College Students: 10-Year Population-Level Trends
     (2007-2017)," *Psychiatric Services*, 70 (2019), 60–63. https://doi.org/10.1176/
     appi.ps.201800332

3   "Timeline: WHO's COVID-19 response," *World Health Organization.* https://
     www.who.int/emergencies/diseases/novel-coronavirus-2019/interactive-timeline

4   "COVID-19 Resources," American College Health Association. https://www.
     acha.org/COVID-19

5   A. M. Campbell, "An increasing risk of family violence during the Covid-19
     pandemic: Strengthening community collaborations to save lives," *Forensic
     Science International: Reports*, (2) Dec. 2020, e-pub ahead of print. https://
     doi.org/10.1016/j.fsir.2020.100089

6   U.S. Department of Housing and Urban Development, Office of Policy Devel-
     opment and Research, "Barriers to success: Housing insecurity for U.S. col-
     lege students," *Insights into housing and community development policy*
     (2015). https://www.huduser.gov/portal/periodicals/insight/insight_2.pdf

7   S. K. Lipson, E. G. Lattie, D. Eisenberg, "Increased rates of mental health
     service utilization by U.S. college students: 10-year population-level trends
     (2007–2017)," *Psychiatric Services* 70(1), (2018), 60–63. https://doi.org/10.1176/
     appi.ps.201800332

8   J. C. Turner, E. V. Leno, A. Keller, "Causes of mortality among American col-
     lege students: A pilot study," *Journal of College Student Psychotherapy* 27(1),
     (2013), 31–42. https://www.ncbi.nlm.nih.gov/pmc/articles/PMC4535338/

9   Healthy Minds Network and American College Health Association, "The impact of COVID-19 on college student well-being," (2020). https://www.acha. org/documents/ncha/Healthy_Minds_NCHaCOVID_Survey_Report_FINAL.pdf J. Xiong, O. Lipsitz, F. Nasri, L.M.W. Lui, H. Gill, L. Phan, D. Chen-Li, M. Iacobucci, R. Ho, A. Majeed, R.S. McIntyre, "Impact of COVID-19 pandemic on mental health in the general population: A systematic review," *Journal of Affective Disorders*, 277 (2020), pp. 55–64. https://doi.org/10.1016/j. jad.2020.08.001

10   Q. H. Chew, K. C. Wei, S. Vasoo, H. C. Chua, and K. Sim, "Narrative synthesis of psychological and coping responses towards emerging infectious disease outbreaks in the general population: Practical considerations for the COVID-19 pandemic," *Singapore Medical Journal* 61(7), (2020), 350–356. https://doi.org/ 10.11622/smedj.2020046
A. Maddrell, "Bereavement, grief, and consolation: Emotional-affective geographies of loss during COVID-19," *Dialogues in Human Geography*, 10(2), 2020, pp. 107–111. https://doi.org/10.1177/2043820620934947

11   A. Kecojevic, C. H. Basch, M. Sullivan, and N. K. Davi, "The impact of the COVID-19 epidemic on mental health of undergraduate students in New Jersey, cross-sectional study," *PLOS One* 15(9), (2020), e0239696. https://doi.org/ 10.1371/journal.pone.0239696

12   Kecojevic, et al.

13   E. H. Sirrine, O. Kliner, and T. J. Gollery, "College student experiences of grief and loss amid the COVID-19 global pandemic," *Omega* (2021): 302228211027461. https://doi.org/10.1177/00302228211027461

14   Sirrine, Kliner, and Gollery.

15   D. L. Mercer and J. M. Evans, "The impact of multiple losses on the grieving process: An exploratory study," *Journal of Loss and Trauma* 11(3), (2006), 219–227. https://doi.org/10.1080/15325020500494178

16   C. D. Chugani and A. Houtrow, "Effect of the COVID-19 pandemic on college students with disabilities," *American Journal of Public Health* 110(12), (2020), 1722–1723. https://doi.org/10.2105/AJPH.2020.305983

17   S. Scott and K. Aquino, "COVID-19 Transitions: Higher Education Professionals' Perspectives on Access Barriers, Services, and Solutions for Students with Disabilities," *Association on Higher Education and Disability* (2020). https:// higherlogicdownload.s3.amazonaws.com/AHEAD/38b602f4-ec53-451c-9be0- 5c0bf5d27c0a/UploadedImages/COVID-19_/AHEAD_COVID_Survey_Report_ Barriers_and_Resource_Needs__2_.docx

18   Chugani and Houtrow.

19   Chugani and Houtrow.

20   K. Raue and L. Lewis, "Students with disabilities at degree-granting postsecondary institutions: First look (NCES 2011-018)," National Center for Education Statistics, US Department of Education (2011). https://eric.ed.gov/?id_ED520976

21   S. P. Choy, "Findings from the condition of education 2002: Nontraditional undergraduates (NCES 2002–012)," National Center for Education Statistics, US Department of Education (2002). https://nces.ed.gov/pubs2002/2002012.pdf; A. W. Radford, M. Cominole, and P. Skomsvold, "Demographic and enrollment characteristics of nontraditional undergraduates: 2011–12 (NCES 2015-025)," Web Tables, US Department of Education, National Center for Education Statistics (2015). https://nces.ed.gov/pubs2015/2015025.pdf

22   S. J. Babb, K. A. Rufino, and R. M. Johnson, "Assessing the effects of the COVID-19 pandemic on nontraditional students' mental health and well-being," *Adult Education Quarterly* (2021). https://doi.org/10.1177/07417136211027508

23   R. C. Trenz, L. Ecklund-Flores, and K. Rapoza, "A comparison of mental health and alcohol use between traditional and nontraditional students," *Journal of American College Health* 63(8), (2015), 584–588. https://doi.org/10.1080/07448481.2015.1040409

24   J. McFarland, B. Hussar, J. Zhang, X. Wang, K. Wang, S. Hein, M. Diliberti, E. Forrest Cataldi, F. Bullock Mann, and A. Barmer, "The condition of education 2019 (NCES 2019-144)," US Department of Education, National Center for Education Statistics (2019). https://nces.ed.gov/pubs2019/2019144.pdf

25   J. K. Giancola, M. J. Grawitch, and D. Borchert, "Dealing with the stress of college: A model for adult students," *Adult Education Quarterly* 59(3), (2009), 246–263. https://doi.org/10.1177/0741713609331479

26   Babb, Rufino, and Johnson.

27   Sirrine, Kliner, and Gollery.

CHAPTER 13: TRANSFORM AND EMANCIPATE SCIENTIFIC LITERACY

1   Pope Francis and Austen Ivereigh, *Let Us Dream: the path to a better future* (New York: Simon & Schuster, 2020), 6.

2   International Commission on the Futures of Education, "Education in a post-COVID world: nine ideas for public action," *UNESCO* (2020), 6. https://unesdoc.unesco.org/ark:/48223/pf0000373717/PDF/373717eng.pdf.multi

3   G. S. Aikenhead, *Science education for everyday life: evidence-based practice* (New York: Teachers College Press, 2006).

4   R. Bybee, "Scientific literacy," in R. Gunstone, ed., *Encyclopedia of science education* (New York: Springer, 2016), 944–946.

5   L. Valladares, "Scientific Literacy and Social Transformation," *Science & Education* 30 (2021), 557–587. https://doi.org/10.1007/s11191-021-00205-2

6   G. S. Aikenhead, "Expanding the research agenda for scientific literacy," in C. Linder, L. Östman, and P.-O. Wickman, eds., *Promoting scientific literacy: Science education research in transaction* (Uppsala, Sweden: Geotryckeriet Uppsala, 2007), 64–71. J.

Sjöström and I. Eilks, "Reconsidering different visions of scientific literacy and science education based on the concept of *Bildung*," in Y. J. Dori, Z. R. Mevarech, and D. R. Baker, eds., *Cognition, Metacognition, and Culture in STEM Education* (New York: Springer, 2018), 65–88.

7   P. Freire, M.B. Ramos, *Pedagogy of the oppressed* (New York: Continuum, 1970).

8   Sjöström and Eilks, 82.

9   National Research Council, *A Framework for K-12 Science Education: Practices, Crosscutting Concepts, and Core Ideas* (Washington, DC: National Academies Press, 2012). https://doi.org/10.17226/13165 ;

National Research Council, *Next Generation Science Standards: For States, By States* (Washington, DC: National Academies Press, 2013). https://doi.org/10.17226/18290

10   National Research Council, *Framework*, 210.

11   G. S. Aikenhead, "What is STS science teaching?" in J. Solomon and G. S. Aikenhead, eds., *STS Education: International Perspectives on Reform* (New York: Teachers College Press, 1994).

12   E. Pedretti and Y. Nazir, "Currents in STSE education: mapping a complex field," *Science Education* 95(4), (2011), 601–626.

13   Pope Francis and Ivereigh, *Let Us Dream*, 35.

14   Pope Francis and Ivereigh, *Let Us Dream*, 7.

15   Valladares.

CHAPTER 14: POPE FRANCIS ON PERSON-CENTERED EDUCATION

1   Pope Francis, *Fratelli Tutti*, United States Conference of Catholic Bishops (2020), no. 99.

2   R. Chatterjee and C. Wroth, "COVID deaths leave thousands of U.S. kids grieving parents or primary caregivers," NPR, October 7, 2021. https://www.npr.org/sections/health-shots/2021/10/07/1043881136/covid-deaths-leave-thousands-of-u-s-kids-grieving-parents-or-primary-caregivers

3   "Education in a pandemic: The disparate impact of COVID-19 on America's students," US Department of Education: Office of Civil Rights, 2021. https://www2.ed.gov/about/offices/list/ocr/docs/20210608-impacts-of-covid19.pdf

4   Pope Francis, "Educating to Fraternal Humanism," Congregation for Catholic Education (Vatican, 2017), no. 8. https://www.vatican.va/roman_curia/congregations/ccatheduc/documents/rc_con_ccatheduc_doc_20170416_educare-umanesimo-solidale_en.html

5   Pope Paul VI, *Progressio Populorum* (Vatican, 1967), no. 87. https://www.vatican.va/roman_curia/congregations/ccatheduc/documents/rc_con_ccathed uc_doc_20170416_educare-umanesimo-solidale_en.html

6   Pope Francis, "Educating to Fraternal Humanism," no. 12.

7   Pope Francis, "Video message of His Holiness Pope Francis on the occasion of the meeting organized by the Congregation for Catholic Education: 'Global compact on education. Together to look beyond,'" (Vatican, 2020). https://www.vatican.va/content/francesco/en/messages/pont-messages/2020/documents/papa-francesco_20201015_videomessaggio-global-compact.html

8   Pope Francis, *Fratelli Tutti*, no. 32.

9   B. Wall, "The concept of nature from Rerum novarum to Laudato si," in B. F. Wall and M. Faggioli, eds., *Pope Francis: A voice of mercy, justice, love, and care for the earth* (Maryknoll, NY: Orbis, 2019), 196.

10 Pope Francis, *Fratelli Tutti*, no. 146.

11 Pope Francis, "Educating to Fraternal Humanism," no. 8.

12 Pope Francis, *Laudato Si*, United States Conference of Bishops (2015), no. 15.

13 Pope Francis, *Laudato Si*, nos. 70, 91, 92.

14 Pope Francis, *Laudato Si*, no. 137.

15 Wall, "The concept of nature," 196.

16 J. I. Kureethadam, *The ten green commandments of Laudato si* (Collegeville, MN: Liturgical Press, 2019), 151.

17 Pope Francis, *Laudato Si*, no. 214.

18 Pope Francis, *Fratelli Tutti*, no. 86.

19 K. Heinz Neufeld, "Spirituality," in W. Beinert and F. S. Fiorenza, eds., *Handbook of Catholic Theology* (New York: Crossroad, 1995), 673-676.

20 Pope Francis, *Fratelli Tutti*, no. 222.

21 Pope Francis, *Fratelli Tutti*, no. 224.

22 W. M. Wright and J. F. Power, *Francis de Sales, Jane de Chantal: Letters of spiritual direction* (Mahwah, NJ: Paulist, 1988), 58.

23 Pope Francis, *Fratelli Tutti*, no. 215.

24 J. Sudbrack, "Spirituality," in K. Rahner, C. Ernst, and K. Smyth, eds., *Sacramentum mundi: An encyclopedia of theology* (New York: Herder and Herder, 1970), 156.

25 J. Tobin, "Flight or field hospital?" in B. F. Wall and M. Faggioli, eds., *Pope Francis: A voice of mercy, justice, love, and care for the earth* (Maryknoll, NY: Orbis, 2019), 8.